Someday Is Not a Plan

A Guide to
Understanding Money
in Plain English

Someday Is Not a Plan

A Guide to
Understanding Money
in Plain English

Dave Straube

Island Eye, LLC

Island Eye, LLC
1500 SW 11th Ave.
Suite 2204
Portland, OR 97201

www.SomedayIsNotaPlan.com

This publication is intended to provide competent and reliable information regarding the subject matter covered. However, it is sold with the understanding that the author and publisher are not engaged in rendering financial, tax, legal, or other professional advice. Laws and practices often vary from state to state and if legal, financial, or other expert assistance is required, the services of a professional should be sought. The author and publisher specifically disclaim any liability that is incurred from the use or application of the contents of this book.

ISBN: 978-0-9747624-3-2

To Kate and Lindsay

Look at it this way...

Table of Contents

Roger and Larry

>> ROGER <<

Family is just as often a curse as a blessing. My brother wants me to talk to his kid, help him get his act together. Funny! It's not as though I was a poster child for good attitude and responsibility at that age. Arrested development was more like it. Fortunately, I've changed over the years. Now I'm your typical 58-year-old retiree checking his investments online, volunteering at a variety of eco-friendly charities, and traveling the country in my quest to run a marathon in every state. But you never would have guessed it had you met me 40 years ago.

It would be nice to blame my folks for my early sins, but the truth is that they were caring, loving parents. I just had my own agenda back then. I had no interest in sports, hobbies, books, Boy Scouts, or anything the least bit productive. It drove my parents nuts, which thrilled me to no end at the time but I've since come to regret. High school passed in a daze. Sure, I can recite the Pythagorean theorem and know that Columbus sailed the ocean blue in 1492, but that's about it. All that other stuff about forms of government, grammar, tangents to a curve, and why Socrates was forced to drink hemlock never sank in. I must have missed class that day.

After high school I had a few manual labor jobs, then enlisted in the Army. Boot camp did not straighten me out. Neither did two years of calisthenics, saluting, and diesel repair. Afterward, I drifted back to my old jobs while many of my service buddies went to college on the G.I. Bill. Using my brain instead of my body hadn't registered as a legitimate and preferable lifestyle yet. But landscaping and construction started to take their toll. Chronic pain has a way of heightening awareness and I began to look for alternatives. What job offered lots of fresh air, no seasonal layoffs, medical benefits, and a pension, I wondered? Ding ding ding! Postal carrier.

The civil service exam didn't succumb to my superior intellect until the third try, but better late than never, I guess. By Christmas of 1973 I was dressed in blue, pushing a tricycle cart, and delivering holiday greetings. Things were looking good. For the first time in my life I had a steady job, had met a nice girl, and much to my surprise, occasionally pondered the future. Twenty-two years old and I was starting to grow up. About time.

One benefit of delivering the mail is that you run across lots of interesting reading material. I couldn't help but notice how *Business Week*, *Forbes*, *Entrepreneur*, and similar periodicals went to the better neighborhoods. There wasn't any proof that reading *Forbes* guaranteed you a higher income. But it sure seemed logical that I should start reading what the well-off folk read if I ever wanted to be well-off myself.

That observation started a multi-year program of financial self-education which hasn't stopped yet. During the day I delivered the mail, and as the years went by, advanced to window clerk and then supervisor. At night I'd head to the library to read the same periodicals I had just delivered to the better neighborhoods. At first I didn't understand a thing and my nightly reading was more an exercise in frustration than anything else.

Maybe it was my desire to earn easy money that made me stick with it, but eventually it started to make sense. As my knowledge grew, I began to see how much of the finance world was just hype and that except for a lucky few, there was no easy money to be had. But the good news was that basic finance was not rocket science. Everyone had a chance at financial security if they understood the basics and were willing to sacrifice today for a better tomorrow.

Of course, there's a big difference between knowing what you should do and actually doing it. It took me a few more years to change my habits, but I've been practicing good finance for 30 years now and things are looking pretty good. My hot-shot lawyer brother doesn't like to admit that I, the lowly civil servant, am far better off than he is. It just goes to show that it's not what you make, it's what you do with it.

I suppose that's why he wants me to talk to his kid. The acorn doesn't fall far from the tree, which would mean the kid hasn't got a clue about money. And if he's got half the attitude I did at his age, he won't want to listen to me. What the heck, he's family. I'll give it a try.

>> LARRY <<

I'm going to barf if my dad tells me once more how much harder he had it at my age. What does he know? Jobs are scarce. Everything is expensive. I'm seriously in debt. He should be glad I'm not living at home like lots of my friends. I've actually got a job and live on my own.

He keeps reminding me how at 26 he was already married, working two jobs, and going to night school. Does he even see how crummy his life is now? He spends all his time at the office, is on cholesterol medication, argues with Mom, and would probably throw out his back if he ever tried to use the custom clubs he got for Christmas two years ago. At least I know how to have fun.

His latest is that I should have a talk with Uncle Roger about my finances. Like that makes a lot of sense. How rich can you get working for the Post Office? Maybe the postmaster general is raking it in, but a branch office supervisor? I don't think so.

That's not to say I couldn't use some money help. Just last week I was out for pizza with the guys and ran into trouble. My card was over the limit and the charge was denied. Fortunately, I had just paid the minimum on my other card and was able to use it there. It sure would be nice to charge stuff without worrying about whether it would go through or not.

I suppose I could have majored in something with better income prospects than architecture. I really believed the hype that if you do something you love, you won't work a day in your life. Ha! Some weeks I'm nothing more than a draftsman, though at least now it's all done on the computer rather than with pencil and eraser. And don't even get me started on scale models. I think I'm developing an allergy to Styrofoam from handling it so much. My boss says I'll get better stuff to do once I pass the Architect Registration Exam. I keep intending to sign up for the review course, but there's always something else going on. What's the rush?

The partners who started the company seem to be doing well. At least they drive decent cars and live in a nice part of town. But I just can't see myself getting there at the rate I'm going. I've been out of school four years now and seem to be struggling just as much as ever. Now, I'm not edging up on 50 like those guys, but still, where is the money supposed to come from? I just don't see it. After rent, car payments, student loans, credit card bills, cable TV, phone plan, food, and incidentals, there's always too much month at the end of the money. How does anyone get ahead these days?

Uncle Roger said coffee was on him, so I guess there's no harm in hearing what he has to say. And he's a lot mellower than my dad. Maybe it's because he's already retired and has less stress in his life. The guy is sort of a mystery, actually. Retired early, travels all the time, and lives in a downtown condo with a killer view. What's he know that I don't?

Making a Plan

Roger was well into the business section of the paper when Larry arrived at Peet's Coffee on the corner of Broadway and Washington. Portland, Oregon, might not be the coffee capital of the world, but it sure was trying. Roger had picked Peet's for their meeting, figuring it would be easy to find. Unlike Starbucks, which could be found on every other corner, this was the only Peet's in the area.

Larry was rumpled but obviously dressed for work in khakis and collared shirt. Roger wore his usual uniform of jeans, non-logo tee, and well-worn running shoes retired from active workout duty. Larry was relieved to see that Roger wore low-cut ankle socks rather than the knee-highs which just shouted "Geezer alert!"

"Good to see you," said Roger as they shook hands. "What'll you have?"

"Double tall no foam latte ought to do it," replied Larry, who needed to jump-start his day.

Roger headed off to the counter while Larry checked out the sports page. He knew most of the scores already as he subscribed to the sports cable package, but it never hurt to see what the print media had to say. Roger returned with their orders a few minutes later and each took a tentative sip as they looked at each other expectantly.

"So, here we are," opened Roger.

"Um, yeah," was all Larry could respond with. After all, it was early yet and most of his latte was still in the cup.

"My brother asked me to talk to you about money. What do you want to know?"

This was starting out poorly already as far as Larry was concerned. If he knew what to ask, he would have asked it of someone long ago, right?

"I don't know," started Larry hesitantly. "Long-term I'd like to be rich. Who doesn't? Short-term it would be nice just to get my bills under control."

"Rich is nice," agreed Roger, letting the conversation hang uncomfortably.

Although Larry said he wanted to be rich, it was really just a pipe dream. At this stage in his life, financial considerations were limited to what gadget to buy next and which credit card to use. He had never quantified things in terms of a dollar amount or the effort required to obtain it. Rich was a distant dream universe where he could buy whatever he wanted without consequences.

Roger picked up the conversation again. "When did you want to achieve financial freedom, Larry?"

"Right now would be fine."

"Seriously, did you have a particular age in mind?"

"I hadn't really thought about it much. I mean, I've dreamed about being loaded. But it was just a dream, you know?"

"Well, given your age and education, there's no reason you can't be rich someday. But you'd need a plan. Otherwise you'll just be average—financially, I mean."

"Isn't that what a financial advisor can do for me—create a plan?" Larry asked.

"There are many financial professionals who can help you—stockbrokers, financial planners, accountants, tax experts, and more. But a plan is about you, about your life. Who knows you best? Who cares the most about you? Those professionals provide services for a fee, that's all."

"You mean those folks can't really help me?"

"I'm just being realistic," countered Roger. "A financial professional is human. His first and biggest interest is himself, so that's where he'll invest the most concern and energy. In other words, his own plan comes first. Anything left over is divided among all his clients. So how much concern and truly personalized advice does any one client really get? Not much."

"So what am I supposed to do?" asked Larry. "I don't have any financial training."

"Don't underestimate what you're capable of learning. Your plan has less to do with specific financial moves and more to do with committing to take responsibility for your financial future. It's the difference between dreaming and doing."

"So all I need to do is decide to be rich, and I will?"

"Not quite. To have so much money that you can't spend it all in your lifetime requires luck, extraordinary talents, or both. But you can achieve financial comfort if you're committed to doing so."

"You make it sound easy."

"Oh, it isn't easy. It requires diligence and tough choices, which is why so few people achieve financial independence. But it isn't complicated. The average Joe can become pretty wealthy with planning and perseverance."

Conversation lapsed while Larry dreamed of high-priced purchases and a matching lifestyle. First on the list would be a Mercedes 450 SL sports car. Lots of guys claimed it was a ladies car, but then what better way to attract them? Next would be a top-floor condo in an exclusive building with views in all directions. Lastly, there would be the ski trips to British Columbia, snorkeling trips to Hawaii, and always with a beautiful woman at his side, naturally.

Roger interrupted his reverie as though reading his mind. "No plan, no good life."

Deep down, Larry knew this was true. In an unusual show of initiative, he asked, "How do I make a plan?"

"Your plan is a very personal thing and you're the only one who can put it together. People forget this, which is why they often don't follow plans someone else put together for them, even at great expense. The good news is that your plan will reveal itself once you know enough financial basics and start being honest with yourself."

"What basics do I need to know?"

"Simple stuff, really. Mostly it's a way of looking at things and understanding their importance. For example, have you ever done a lifetime earnings calculation?"

"A what?"

"A lifetime earnings calculation," said Roger slowly. "That's where you calculate how much money you're going to earn in your lifetime."

"Nope, never did one of those."

"We'll do a simplistic one for you so you see how it works. Let's say your salary was $25,000 per year and you were going to work 40 years, from age 25 to 65. Assuming you never got a raise, how much money would you make in your lifetime?"

"One million dollars," said Larry after some quick mental math.

"As you gain experience, you can expect a few raises during your career. With even modest increases, two million dollars will pass through your hands in your lifetime."

"Wow, that's serious money!"

"And if you're exceptionally talented and a little bit lucky, your lifetime earnings might be significantly more."

Larry tried to comprehend the magnitude of two-million-plus dollars, but it was hard to do. Numbers that big just didn't have any basis in reality. At least not his reality.

"Now let's say you saved 10% of your salary each year," continued Roger. "Even if it never earned a cent of interest, how much would you have at age 65?"

"Well," said Larry, "10% of two million is $200,000. But there's no way I could save 10% of my salary each year. I'm just barely paying the bills as it is."

"Yes, that's how a financial loser thinks."

Larry couldn't believe Roger had just insulted him. "What?"

"That was a bit harsh, I guess," responded Roger. "But financial losers always have a reason why they can't save money or bring their financial lives under control."

"And I'm a financial loser because I don't save 10% of my salary each year?" asked Larry heatedly. "I've got student loans to pay off and lots of other bills besides. You don't know a thing about my finances."

"Easy there," cautioned Roger. "You're right that I don't know much about your finances, but I'm pretty sure you could be setting aside 10% every year."

"No way."

"You've been out of school how many years?"

"Four."

"Has your salary increased by 10% since you started at your company?"

"Better than that, even," answered Larry.

"And when you first started working, were you paying your student loans, eating well, and living comfortably?"

"Oh yeah. It was great to be earning some real money."

"Couldn't you have saved those raises instead of spending them?"

"Sure, but where's the fun in that? I earned those raises. I deserve to spend them."

"You need to look at it differently. You've put in four years of hard work and not only do you have nothing saved, I suspect you've got more debt than you started with and aren't any happier. What's wrong with this picture?"

Larry was reluctant to admit it, but Roger was right. Life just wasn't as much fun now as it had been when he first got out of school. Back then, everything was new—new job, new city, new friends. Sure, he lived in a nicer apartment now, had a better car, and could afford more toys, thanks to the increased limits on his credit cards. But the fun was gone. His time was spent at work, watching TV, or spending. And Roger had guessed correctly about the debt. After college, Larry's only debt had been the student loan. Now he was saddled with a hefty car loan and he'd only been paying the minimums on his credit cards for months.

The lack of a comeback told Roger he had hit the mark. He held out an olive branch of sorts. "You don't need to save every raise for the rest of your life, you know. Just commit to saving the next set of raises until your salary has risen another 10%. You do this by spending the same as you do now and placing any rise in income into a savings account. This establishes a savings rate. After you hit the 10% mark, you can start spending raises again, provided you maintain the savings rate. A one-time deferment of pleasure sets you up for a lifetime of savings. What could be easier than that?"

"Sounds reasonable," said Larry, "but I've got such a long list of stuff I want. And then there's the bills..."

"Aren't you capable of more than lusting after the next shining bauble? Who's in control of your life?"

"Well, I am, I guess. It's just that..."

"...it's so hard to do the right thing?" finished Roger for him.

"Right!"

"That's how most people feel. In fact, they feel bad about themselves because they know it's their decision to spend instead of save. But they feel helpless to change. As a result, they end up in a continual cycle of spending followed by self-recrimination."

"Ugh, who wants to do that for 40 years?"

"Good question, but so many do."

"So how do I break the cycle?" asked Larry.

"That's where your plan comes in. You need a plan that's more attractive to you than the quick rush provided by the next purchase. With a plan, your actions start to have meaning and you have a chance, just barely a chance, to control your financial destiny."

"I understand what you're saying, but I still don't know how to make my plan. I don't even know where to begin."

"That's completely normal for someone your age starting out in life. Remember when I said earlier that your plan will reveal itself once you have some rudimentary financial knowledge and start being honest with yourself?"

"Yes."

"You have to have faith that that's really how it works. Don't worry about the plan for now. Educate yourself. The plan will follow."

"How do I do that?"

"How indeed?" replied Roger, a smile on his face. "Maybe that's a good topic for next time."

Free Money

Larry had debated long and hard whether to meet Roger a second time. Getting a free coffee was nice, but certainly not at the expense of being called a financial loser. His uncle seemed like a bit of a flake, too. All that talk about needing a plan while at the same time not worrying about a plan. That was supposed to be financial advice?

Regardless, the seed Roger had planted in Larry's mind about saving 10% of his salary had taken root. He wasn't ready to actually do that yet. But intuitively he knew that to grow small money into bigger money, you had to have the small money to begin with. And the only logical place to get it was by saving some of his salary.

This time they were meeting at Stumptown Coffee, just around the corner from their last meeting place. Stumptown's name reflected Portland's roots in logging country and was known for serving only fair trade coffee and having a massage therapist on the payroll. In recent years it had taken on outside investors, become a Delaware corporation, and opened shops in Seattle and New York City. That didn't seem to have hurt its popularity any, though.

Roger had staked out two places in the lounge area for their talk. He was on one end of the 20-foot sectional that paralleled two walls of the room. His bag claimed the easy chair set 90 degrees off from him, which would make conversation easy. Larry came in shortly and was surprised to see Roger had his regular waiting for him.

"Great service!" lauded Larry as he moved the bag and settled in.

"Didn't want to fight the line twice, that's all. Been doing any thinking about what we talked about last time?"

"I don't have a plan, if that's what you're asking."

"Early for that, definitely."

"But I have been thinking about investing."

"Did you find some money in the couch?" wisecracked Roger.

That comment wouldn't have had much effect coming from one of Larry's buddies. But for some reason he couldn't identify, coming from Roger it really got under his skin and he considered telling him to stuff it and walking out. But he didn't need to be at work for a bit yet and his latte wasn't in a paper cup he could grab and go. Larry

11

took a deep breath and considered how he might extract some useful information from Roger as painlessly as possible.

"Let's say I did manage to save 10% of my salary. Who can help me invest it so that it grows the fastest?" asked Larry.

"There's lots of stockbrokers and financial advisors who would love to generate some fees off you. But the first thing they'll ask is what risk you're willing to assume."

"Risk?"

"And then they'll try to sound smart by yapping about beta."

"Beta? What's that?"

"Beta is the measure of a stock's volatility in relation to the overall market. The stock market as a whole is defined as having a beta of one. A beta over one means a stock is more volatile than the market. A beta under one means a stock has less volatility than the market. So beta is essentially the sensitivity of a stock's return to the market return."

"What a bunch of gobbledygook. I just want to know what to invest in. Can't the stockbroker tell me that?"

Roger couldn't suppress a laugh.

"What's so funny?" challenged Larry.

"If stockbrokers knew the best investments," answered Roger, "they wouldn't need to work as stockbrokers anymore. They could just relax in their mansions, call in a wise investment now and then, and reap the rewards of their omniscience. It's wishful thinking to believe an advisor can hand out investing silver bullets."

"I know, I know. I need to educate myself first."

"You're off to a good start by asking questions," consoled Roger. "Risk is actually a very simple concept."

"It is?"

"Sure. Suppose some random guy on the street said he could double your money overnight. Would you loan him your savings?"

"Heck, no!"

"That's right. And the reason is that the guy represents a risk. You don't know if you're going to get your money back at all, much less doubled. Investments work exactly the same way. Usually the ones with the biggest potential return also have the largest risk. More sedate investments return less, but you can sleep nights because you know you'll get your money back."

"That's simple. So why all the beta business?"

"Beta is an effective tool for managing a portfolio of stocks. But until you actually have a portfolio of stocks, you don't need to worry about it."

Larry thought about Roger's method for working up to a 10% savings rate. If he'd done that from day one, he'd now have a nest egg of $10,000. Granted, the DVD collection wouldn't be as deep and he might still be watching the old TV rather than the wide-screen. But $10,000? That would cover a serious entertainment setup and then some! Maybe there was something to this savings business.

"Thinking what $10,000 would buy?" asked Roger.

"How did you know I was thinking about that?" asked a surprised Larry.

"Just an educated guess," replied Roger. "I figured your salary at around $25,000 per year. Ten percent saved each year for four years comes to $10,000. We're not talking pocket change anymore, are we?"

"Definitely not. I could make a serious dent in my wish list with that."

"No doubt. But most people's wish lists grow just as fast as their savings. Until they learn about free money, that is."

"Free money? This I've got to hear."

"I suppose it isn't free in the strictest sense of the word. But it is pretty close."

"Are you going to tell me or not?" asked Larry anxiously.

"Well, it's going to cost you..."

"I knew there was a catch!"

"Just kidding. You've no doubt heard the saying 'Time is money,' right?"

"Sure, everyone knows that one."

"Most people think it has to do with getting busy, that time is a precious resource which shouldn't be wasted."

"That's not what it means?"

"That's one interpretation. The other interpretation is best illustrated with an example. Let's say you wanted to buy something but didn't have the money for it. You have two options. One is to start saving and wait until you have enough money to make the purchase. The other is to find someone to lend you the money so you can make the purchase now, along with your promise to pay them back later."

"I'm following, but where's the free money?"

"We're getting there. Think about the person lending you the money. Haven't they been inconvenienced? After all, they did the hard work of saving but instead of getting to spend it, they lent it to you."

"There's a fool born every minute, right?"

"True, but I suspect we're not thinking of the same fool here. The lender will want to be compensated for his inconvenience. So you, the borrower, have to pay back the original amount plus some extra, typically called interest."

Larry couldn't believe Roger was making such a big deal of this. Of course, he would have to pay interest when he borrowed money. Who didn't? "I still don't see where the free money comes in."

"That's because you only know yourself as a borrower. Imagine you had saved up the $10,000 and now you lent it to someone else for a year at 5% interest. How much would you be repaid when the year is up?"

"That's easy. The original $10,000 plus the 5% interest for a total of $10,500."

"Very good. Now what did you have to do to earn that extra $500?"

"Nothing!" exclaimed Larry, finally seeing the light.

"Free money," pointed out Roger. "I rest my case."

The image of free money was beginning to intrigue Larry. He had never considered being a lender, much less profiting from it. Money had always been a scarce resource that needed to be earned, spent, or paid back. Saving, lending, and profiting were new and attractive concepts. Best of all, the system only required patience— and a reliable person to lend to. Now there was a problem. The idea of threatening to break someone's kneecaps unless they paid up didn't sound too appealing. Where did one find reliable people to lend to?

"Where do I find a reliable borrower?" asked Larry.

"Lend your money to a bank."

"That's not how it works," pointed out Larry archly. "People borrow money from banks, not the other way around."

"Then where do banks get their money from?" asked Roger. "They're not printing it in the basement."

"Probably not."

"Banks don't have money of their own, they just manage other people's money. When you deposit money in your savings account, you're lending it to the bank. In return, they pay you interest. The bank then turns around and lends your money to someone else at a higher rate of interest. As long as the interest spread covers the cost of running the bank, they make money. That's a simplified view of things, but it captures the gist of it."

"So the bank is just a middleman between me and the person borrowing my money," summarized Larry in a flash of understanding. "How do I know the bank will pay me back?"

"That's a good question. Always understand your risk. Banks, at least most of them, are insured by the FDIC, the Federal Deposit Insurance Corporation. The FDIC currently insures the first $250,000 you have on deposit at a bank. So the money you lend to the bank is guaranteed up to $250,000, even if whoever the bank loaned your money to doesn't pay up."

"Sounds pretty good. But my savings account only pays 1% interest. I'll never get rich at that rate."

"You're coming along nicely, Larry. First you analyze the risk. Now you're looking at the return. There's hope yet!" razzed Roger. "View your savings account as a safe place to accumulate an initial set of funds while you educate yourself. Over time, you'll learn about other free money opportunities which pay more, but have more risk or require more money up front."

This was getting to be too much for Larry. Lending instead of spending. Banks borrowing from people. Free money. What was next?

"Do you know how long it would take to double your money at 2% interest?" asked Roger.

"I don't know, ten years maybe?"

"Try thirty-six."

"Thirty-six years! That's forever."

"That's why a savings account is just the starting point. But the reason I asked is so I could tell you about the Rule of 72."

"Never heard of that one."

"Uh huh. College degree in architecture but doesn't even know the simplest rule of thumb in finance. There's an indictment of the American educational system if I ever heard one. Regardless, the Rule of 72 tells you how long it would take to double your money at any given interest rate. Just divide the interest rate into 72 to get the approximate number of years to double your money."

"That's simple enough. If I could find someone paying 10% interest, I could turn my $10,000 into $20,000 in seven years just by sitting around and waiting."

"And don't forget, the first $10,000 was your money. The second $10,000 was what again?"

"Free money!" filled in Larry on cue. "I'm starting to get the hang of this."

Larry checked his watch a second time and Roger knew it must be time for him to get to work. Time to bring today's lesson to a close.

"You must be pretty good at math if you're designing buildings and such," offered Roger.

"There is a fair bit of math involved," agreed Larry, "but most of it is pretty straightforward. If you can look up load factors in tables, add and multiply, you've got most of it covered."

"I'm surprised, then, that you didn't question the Rule of 72 as applied to your hypothetical $10,000 at 10% interest."

"What do you mean?"

"You're the math guy. Work it out. Ten percent of $10,000 is $1,000 per year. Over seven years that makes $7,000. Added to the original amount, you end up with $17,000 after seven years, not $20,000. Where's the catch?"

"You said the rule was just an approximation."

"I don't think the rule would be popular if it were that far off the mark," said Roger, shaking his head. "Think about it some more."

Larry hated mental exercises like these. There was always some misleading detail that led you to a wrong answer. But he could find nothing amiss with the calculation. "I don't see it," he conceded.

"Do the calculation for just the first year then," suggested Roger.

"All right. We start with $10,000 and in the first year earn 10% which equals $1,000. So at the end of the first year we have $11,000."

"You're doing great. Now do the calculation for the second year."

"Well, we start with the $11,000 from the end of the first year and earn 10% which equals $1,100. Oh, I see it now!" said Larry brightly. "It grows faster every subsequent year because the free

16

money from the year before earns more new free money of its own. What a scam!"

"You may call it a scam. The rest of us call it compound interest and it is the driving force behind wealth creation. As long as there are borrowers out there, and it doesn't look like we'll run out of them anytime soon, you can turn one dollar into two without lifting a finger. Just sit back and wait and compound interest will do the work for you."

"Why doesn't everybody know about this?"

"Many people do know about it, but they don't have the discipline to get started or the patience to stick with it. Remember, it only works if you have something saved to lend. Only then can you get on the free money gravy train. At some point, you have to decide whether you want to go through life as a borrower or as a lender. Only the lenders get the free money."

Demon Debt

Larry was a minimalist when it came to effort, so the idea of free money was attractive. It was almost as though you were getting something for nothing. No wonder there were so many banks. What a great business concept! Borrow money at 2% and lend it back out at 8%. He should have gone into banking instead of architecture. The hours were better and he'd get paid for reading the *Wall Street Journal* all morning. Well, it was too late to become a banker and in all likelihood, it was the people who owned the bank who were enjoying the free money. The ones who worked there were probably wage slaves just like him. But if he could save up a bit and find some of the high-interest investments Roger had hinted at, then he could start enjoying some free money too. The only problem was, Roger had said one needed a larger initial sum to get the higher interest rates. That would be a problem.

Today's meet was at Caffé Umbria in the Pearl District. Twenty years ago, this area of town was a decaying collection of brick warehouses and manufacturing businesses. Now it was a tribute to the effectiveness of rezoning, tax incentives, and developer enthusiasm. An entirely new ecosystem built around the wants and preferences of young professionals had replaced the old. Organic food outlets, eclectic restaurants, quirky furniture stores, and a surplus of coffee shops catered to the new residents of attractive condo buildings.

Caffé Umbria adhered to the modern style with counters of stainless steel, porcelain tile floors, and gunmetal seating. Baristas could make any drink from Cafe au Lait to Espresso Con Panna and satisfy your food needs with a prosciutto, arugula, and bocconcini grilled panini. This was definitely not one of Roger's usual haunts, but Larry had an appointment around the corner later on and it was only a few blocks from a streetcar stop. The weather was mild so the duo sat outside under the overhang and people-watched before getting to the subject at hand.

"Roger, how much money do I need to have to get in on high-interest deals which pay more than 1%?"

"Good question. That's the kind of thinking which eventually leads to a plan."

"Yeah, but I'm worried I'll be stuck at 1% returns forever. I don't want to wait 72 years to double my money."

"You need less than you might think to achieve better returns. Ever heard of a CD?"

"Sure, great audio quality and lasts forever," joked Larry, "though I suspect you mean a Certificate of Deposit. I've seen signs for them at my bank."

"That's right. A CD is just another way for you to lend your money to the bank. But it comes with conditions."

"Such as?"

"Consider your savings account. You have the right to withdraw all your money anytime you want. What's the bank to do if you want your money back but they lent it to someone else in the meantime?"

"Give me someone else's money that they haven't lent out yet and hope that person doesn't want to make a withdrawal just then?" asked Larry, considering the complexities of juggling the money in thousands of accounts without running short.

"In essence, yes. So you can see that from the bank's point of view, the money lent to them in savings accounts isn't very reliable. A CD is a more reliable source of money because you are lending it to the bank for a specific period of time."

"You mean I'll earn more interest just because I promise not to want it back within, say, a year?"

"That's right. The bank is willing to pay a premium for the guarantee that you won't want your money back prematurely. Conversely the lender, that's you in this case, demands additional compensation for being inconvenienced for a fixed period of time."

"Hey, another twist on 'Time is money'!"

"Yes."

"But what if I have an emergency and really do need the money back early?"

"You mean like a sale on stereo equipment?" asked Roger with a grin.

"No, a real emergency, like a medical bill or something."

"You can cash in a CD early, but then you'll forfeit interest. In general, you shouldn't be buying CDs until you can keep a sufficient supply of emergency money in your savings account at all times. For most people, three months' living expenses is a good target."

Conversation lapsed as they observed the steady stream of customers coming and going. Roger grew up in the era before portable consumer electronics and marveled at how ubiquitous they had become. The person without ear buds, cell phone, or tablet device was a distinct minority. Were "pedestrian hit by car" accidents up, now that so many walked around squinting at a micro-sized screen rather than looking where they were going? And what would happen when this generation's eyesight started going? Roger had evolved with the times and owned his share of devices. But he still preferred to experience his surroundings while making his way through the city rather than sleepwalk in an electronic cocoon. Larry's observations were more befitting a bachelor.

Roger broke the silence. "I never answered your original question."

"What was that?" asked Larry, who had forgotten where the conversation started.

"You asked how much money you need to lend in order to earn a better interest rate. I'll bet you can figure out the answer yourself with what we discussed earlier."

Larry thought out loud. "Well, you keep on talking about compensation for being inconvenienced. Lending a large sum is certainly more inconvenient than lending a small amount, so my guess is that the interest rate rises along with the amount of money a person is willing to lend."

"Very good!" congratulated Roger. "You hit the nail on the head. You can verify that theory by looking at the financial page in the newspaper sometime. You'll notice that CDs have minimum investment amounts. Invariably, the $10,000 CD will pay a higher interest than a $1,000 CD."

"OK, but what interest will they pay? Ten percent?"

"I doubt you'll find any CDs at 10% nowadays, though that has happened in the past during times of high inflation like in the 1980s. But you're looking in the wrong place for high-interest savings. I know where you can earn 15% to 20% on your money right now. And you don't need thousands saved up first."

That got Larry's attention. "I knew there was an easier way than what we've been talking about." Free money without having to save money first. Was Roger finally going to reveal some useful financial secrets?

"Keep your shirt on. You probably won't like what you're about to hear."

"What's not to like? High gain without pain. Sounds like a no-brainer to me."

"It is a no-brainer, yet many folks overlook it. Let me ask you a question. Are you carrying a balance on any of your credit cards?"

Larry didn't like where this was going already. All of his cards were maxed out. He managed his credit card balances like a variety show performer spinning plates on poles. Usually he didn't pay until just a few days before the bill was due, and then only the minimum.

"Sometimes," hedged Larry.

"Remember," said Roger, noting his reluctance, "honesty is the best policy. You're only fooling yourself if you don't acknowledge the way things really are."

"OK then. Yes. My cards are almost always at their limit."

"Well, the good news, then, is that you have the most to gain. What's the interest rate on your cards?"

"I dunno. Whoever reads those stupid cardmember agreements, anyway?"

"Those contracts are boring reading, I'll grant you that. But the old adage about how 'The bold print giveth and the fine print taketh away' is all too true. You're most likely getting eaten alive by an interest rate near 20%, not to mention late fees and such."

"Don't even get me started on late fees," bellyached Larry.

"If you were the kind of guy who read the fine print, you probably wouldn't be in the mess you're in now, so no sense in trying to change your reading habits. But let me appeal to your sense of logic."

"Sure."

"What would you say if I told you that regardless of what price was listed for an item, I always paid 20% more?"

"That would be pretty stupid."

"It most certainly would be. But if an item doesn't disappear from your card balance within a year, then that's essentially what you're doing. And if you always carry a balance, year in and year out, then the cumulative surcharge you pay for every item could be much higher than 20%."

Larry got it loud and clear that carrying a balance on his credit cards was the equivalent of overpaying for every item he charged. He'd never thought of it that way before, but it made perfect sense. The minute interest kicked in, the price of the item charged went up.

He wasn't sure who he should be mad at—the credit card companies for gouging him or himself for being such a patsy.

"Don't get too down on yourself," said Roger, suspecting Larry was ruing his fondness for buying things on credit.

"If only it weren't so damn convenient to charge stuff."

"Funny you should use the word 'convenient.' Do you see the connection?"

"What connection?"

"Remember when we talked about lending money to the bank? There you were being compensated for the inconvenience of going without your money for a while. With credit cards, you pay extra later for the convenience of buying things with money you don't have now."

"I get it, but it doesn't make it any easier not to charge things."

"I'm not so sure I want to visit a building you designed," ribbed Roger.

"What do you mean?"

"Because you aren't connecting the dots yet. If you design buildings like you run your finances, they must be shaky structures."

"What are you talking about?" Larry asked, wondering where this was coming from.

"Imagine, Larry, that we could make a clone of you identical in all respects except one. You and your clone would have the same desires, earn the same salary, and make the same choices, except for one small difference. Unlike you, your clone wouldn't charge things. He would save the money first and only buy once he had enough saved up."

"OK," said Larry, still wondering what direction this was taking.

"Now think about you versus your clone over the next ten years. He's paying cash for everything while you charge and carry a balance. How much have you been paying for everything?"

"120%?" asked Larry, thinking of ten years' worth of interest charges.

"Exactly. And remember that you both had the same income, in other words, the same amount of money to spend. But you're paying more for everything. Who has more toys?"

"My clone does," said Larry dejectedly, finally seeing the true impact of his charge card habits.

"That's right. And what is it that you have but your clone doesn't?"

Larry couldn't think of anything. If he was paying more for each item than his clone, how could he possibly end up with something his clone didn't? "Give me a hint?" he asked.

"Think of it in terms of what your clone is avoiding, perhaps."

After a few moments, it dawned on him. At the end of the ten years, it wasn't as though his debts were miraculously wiped clean. "I would still have a balance due on my credit cards."

"Exactly. Ten years gone by, less goodies, and still in debt. If that isn't an incentive to change, then I don't know what is."

Know Your Expenses

Larry's mythical clone had been a constant irritation since their last meeting. One minute he would hate his clone for setting such a goody two-shoes example. The next he would hate himself for mismanaging his credit cards so poorly. After all, it was totally obvious that with identical incomes, he who additionally paid interest ended up with less stuff. And unless you were some kind of wacko "less is more" minimalist, wasn't more stuff the object of work to begin with? That's not to say he had changed his habits any yet, but he was thinking about it.

Larry had a tight schedule today, so they were meeting in the Starbucks around the corner from his office. This was the sanctuary he escaped to when he needed a break from work. He knew all the help by name, who had the afternoon shift on Thursdays, and how late he could stop by in the morning without his favorite muffins being sold out yet. His daily tithe to the cleverly marketed corporation helped keep Starbucks in the black, year after year.

"You're a Starbucks fan, are you?" asked Roger.

"Oh yeah, that's definitely one of my vices," said Larry. "I usually get a latte on the way to work and often a little pick-me-up in the afternoon. This place is real convenient."

"How much do you spend here a day then?"

"I don't know. It's just pocket change."

"Humor me," challenged Roger.

"Two lattes a day," considered Larry, "sometimes a muffin. It probably comes to about $7 a day."

"Do you tip? Let's get the full amount here."

"OK, call it eight bucks then."

"Let's say you work fifty weeks a year, what's that add up to?"

"That's an easy one. Eight dollars per day times five days per week is $40, and that times the fifty work weeks per year is... TWO THOUSAND DOLLARS. Wow! That's some serious money."

"Yes, it is," acknowledged Roger somberly.

Larry was temporarily mute, realizing that $2,000 per year represented 8% of his $25,000 annual salary. No wonder he was always short money. But this was for coffee. Wasn't that necessary for survival just like oxygen and food?

"Many people don't realize how much their spending habits are really costing them," stated Roger. "You're probably a bit worse than that in reality if you include weekends, snacks, and that sort of thing. Over the years it really adds up. And it looks even worse if you consider that you're paying with after-tax dollars."

"What do you mean, after-tax dollars?"

"Everything you buy is with the money you have left over after taxes. Take your Starbucks habit, for example. Assuming you pay 20% income tax on average, that means you had to earn ten dollars so that you would have eight dollars left over after taxes for your daily hit. You can't forget about Uncle Sam, you know."

"I guess," said Larry.

"Here's a quiz for you. How much of your annual salary is going toward lattes?"

"Eight percent," responded Larry instantly, proud to have already figured that out previously.

"You're still not getting it," admonished Roger. "Two thousand is what you're spending. But what are you earning in order to have that $2,000 left over after taxes? Assume 20% taxes like before to make the calculation easy."

Larry thought on this for a while. Of course, you always had to pay income tax. Therefore you had to earn more than the listed price of something in order to pay for it. Bummer. Next he turned to Roger's question. If he was paying 20% tax on average, then out of every five dollars he earned, one went to taxes and the remaining four were his to spend. So the $2,000 he spent represented four parts out of the five he needed to earn. If four parts was $2,000, then one part was $500, and the five parts altogether were $2,500.

"I need to earn $2,500 per year in order to spend $8 per day here," summarized Larry.

"And what percentage of your overall salary is that?" asked Roger rhetorically.

"Ten percent," confessed Larry.

"Unwelcome news, huh?"

"For sure."

"Well, there's no reason you shouldn't enjoy your daily fix. But the financially savvy do two things that you're not. First, they understand the true cost of all their expenditures. Second, they pick their expenditures very carefully so that they don't sabotage their

savings and investment plan. The rich don't spend indiscriminately–
–at least not while they're still on the way to becoming rich."

Roger debated how to bring up the next topic because it was one
no one ever wanted to hear.

"You've heard the saying 'Knowledge is power' haven't you?"
asked Roger.

"Everybody knows that one."

"It applies to your finances as well. You're powerless unless
you know where your money is going. How could you possibly
know whether you're fulfilling your plan, assuming you had one, if
you didn't know how you were spending your money?"

"Don't tell me I should carry around a pencil and notebook,
recording every penny I spend," cautioned Larry.

"Yes, you should. At least you should track all your expenses.
Whether you use pencil and notebook is up to you."

"I can't be bothered with all that."

"Suit yourself. But without accurate data, you're digging your
financial grave one purchase at a time."

Deep down Larry knew this was true. But he didn't particularly
want insight into his spending habits because that way he could
avoid accepting responsibility for them. As long as his buying habits
were nebulously poor rather than specifically bad here and here and
here, he could slough off the guilt and continue as before. Tracking
expenses would force him to confront his spending habits on a
regular basis much like those in therapy have to announce 'My name
is whatever and I'm a shopaholic' at the start of each meeting.
Where was the fun in that?

"I suppose you track your expenses," said Larry with an edge.

"Down to the last penny," boasted Roger. "One dollar or one
hundred, I track it."

"Even the small stuff?"

"Sure, it all adds up. Let's say you buy a *USA Today* each day
on the way to work. It's only a buck each time but still $250 per
year. No doubt you make other small purchases which, in sum, total
to several thousand dollars' worth of discretionary spending
annually."

"I see that, but it still seems like such a bother."

"Quit whining and instead figure out a system that works."

"How do you do it?" asked Larry.

"I get receipts with every purchase and enter them in a spreadsheet each night."

"What a pain!"

"Not really. It takes about two minutes a day, that's all."

"I'll bet your spreadsheet automatically generates pie charts and everything," gibed Larry.

"True," conceded Roger sheepishly. "But that's just what works for me. You've got to find what works for you. You're a modern guy with lots of electronic devices, aren't you?"

"I guess."

"Many PDAs, smart phones, and other devices have apps for tracking expenses. As long as you have your device with you, you can enter the data right away. Later you can upload, aggregate, and generate statistics for the month or year."

"I suppose," said Larry, secretly thinking he wasn't about to start punching data into his smart phone app every time he left Starbucks. Heck, both hands were full. One held the latte and the other, the muffin his waistline didn't need!

"Or you could stop using cash."

"How does that help track expenses?"

"If you never use cash, then every purchase you make will be recorded on your credit and debit card statements. In theory, you can reverse engineer a complete picture of your spending from all those statements. But frankly, it seems easier to do a bit each day rather than analyze cryptic statements once a month."

Neither seemed like an attractive alternative to Larry. What was the point? Was a pie chart which showed how much he was spending on designer coffee really going to change anything? What he really needed was more money to begin with. That was much simpler than accounting for every last penny and making a federal case out of whether he bought a newspaper on the way to work or not.

Roger understood the reluctance to track expenses. If it was enjoyable more people would do it, right? The problem was one of faith. If the belief was there, the motivation to act would follow as naturally as night follows day. He took a different approach with his nephew.

"Do you believe that aside from winning the lottery, you need to become a lender or investor to accrue wealth?" asked Roger.

"Or I could just earn more," said Larry.

"That's true, but how's it working for you? You've been steadily earning more since you got out of school, but seem to be deeper in the hole than when you started. I'd wager that earning more hasn't helped one bit."

Larry didn't have an answer to that. Roger continued, "So if that's not the answer, where's the problem?"

"Maybe it is me," admitted Larry after a lengthy pause of self-examination.

"Exactly—but don't take that personally. Being on top of the food chain, constructing the seven wonders of the world, and taming the atom has made us humans think quite highly of ourselves. But despite mankind's achievements collectively, each individual is the weak link in the chain of decisions which define his life."

"Heavy."

"Thank you, even if it isn't an original observation. Back to your situation then, would being less of a spender and more of a lender and investor improve your situation?"

"Probably," granted Larry.

"Then look at it this way. Within any given year, you've only got so much money coming in, right?"

"Right."

"Then to increase the amount available to save or invest, you have to steal it back from what you spend. Still with me?"

"Yes."

"And the only way to do that is to know where you're spending to begin with. Therefore you need to..."

"...track expenses," finished Larry reluctantly.

"Hey, it's not a death sentence," said Roger, noting the resignation in his voice.

"Just about, though. Documenting every last penny would drive me crazy. I'd hate it."

"But if you spend less often just to avoid taking notes on what you spent, then the system is working!"

"Ha, ha."

"Here's another approach. Rather than track every picayune expenditure, allow yourself a fixed amount of pocket money each day. Pay for the little stuff out of that, but record everything else. 'Everything else' may only be one or two items per day—really no big deal to keep track of."

That might work, thought Larry.

"But you need a system to discourage cheating. Let's say you allot $10 per day. Each morning you put exactly $10 in your right pocket. If you can't pay for something out of your right pocket, then your choice is not to buy it or to record the purchase."

This was finally starting to sound reasonable, but $10 didn't get you too far these days. If he bumped it up to $20, it could cover lunch and he wouldn't have to record much of anything except trips to the grocery store. And the ATM spit out twenties, so there was no problem getting the right amount to stick in his pocket each morning.

"That's a plan I could follow."

"Good," said Roger. "But resist the temptation to make the daily amount too big. For example, $20 per work day might eliminate a few receipts, but would be 20% of your salary. That's a lot of money to piddle away unaccounted for."

"How did you know I was thinking of raising the daily amount?"

"It's what I would have done at your age!" replied Roger. "The times may change, but human nature doesn't."

Larry could see where this was headed. First Roger had him tracking every last penny. Next he'd be making a budget—and probably one without as much pizza as he was currently enjoying. There was a certain excitement around earning free money and rolling in riches. But tracking and budgeting? That was geezer manager work. Boring with a capital B.

"I'll bet you're going to tell me about budgeting next, aren't you?" asked Larry.

"Nope. Most people think of budgets as defining what they can't have, rather than what they can. Denial just doesn't work as a motivator."

"Isn't tracking expenses sort of the same thing?"

"Depends. Let's say you really wanted to find some extra money to invest each month, but just can't seem to do it. In that scenario, tracking expenses is a tool to help you find that money. You'll want to do it because it helps you achieve your goal."

"So if I really want extra money each month, then tracking expenses will suddenly be easy and fun? I don't think so!"

Roger knew how Larry felt. There was a certain freedom, if not power, in earning a paycheck and spending at will. Nobody wanted to give that up once they had a taste of it. The problem was that most people went too far. Credit made it too easy to spend more than

100% of one's salary. People on that path were slipping further underwater with each swipe of the card. Some people had enough sense to only spend what they earned, but even that was just treading water. To really get ahead, you had to replace spending with investing.

"I don't claim to be able to make it fun, but you have to keep trying until you find something that works for you," said Roger.

"Like Edison and the light bulb?"

"Exactly. Failure is merely the path of least persistence."

Buy Smart

Roger took a window seat at Seven Virtues Coffeehouse on the Portland east side and wondered whether Larry would show. Perhaps he had misinterpreted Larry's many abbreviations in last night's text message exchange. At one time the phone was heralded as a great leap forward in human communications. As far as Roger was concerned, texting was a step backward as everyone had their private, indecipherable shorthand and the nuance of inflection was lost. Not that it mattered. In a few decades, device-assisted telepathy would be the norm and then the problem would be how to turn it off so you could have a private moment with yourself.

This coffee shop was close to where Larry was dropping off his car for service that morning. Roger had offered to drive him to the office afterward. The seven virtues were a concept from early Catholicism intended to counterbalance the seven deadly sins. The idea was that you protect yourself from each sin by practicing its opposing virtue. For example, practicing temperance protected you from greed, humility from pride, and so on. Each table was stamped with the coffeehouse logo and had one of the virtues written on it. Roger noted that he had picked the "patience" table. He always needed a good dose of that when dealing with his nephew.

A sharp-looking BMW rolled up and Larry extricated himself from the low-slung seats.

"Hey, nice car," commented Roger. "You up-and-coming architects travel in style."

"What do you drive, a Lincoln Town Car?" miffed Larry, suggesting Roger might be too over the hill for a decent ride.

"No, I drive a five-year-old Ford," said Roger simply, noting Larry's sensitivity to being razzed about his car. Better make amends, he decided, before they started off on the wrong foot. "There's nothing wrong with buying value, which the BMW certainly is—as long as you can afford it at your current stage in life and don't overpay."

"Oh, I got a good deal," boasted Larry. "They were able to get the payments down to what I wanted and everything."

Roger suspected Larry got taken to the cleaners but didn't want to rile his nephew any further. "I'm sure you did," he said as neutrally as possible.

31

Larry could tell Roger was holding something back. "What? What is it? You don't think I got a good deal?"

"I don't know the details of your deal. But 'what payment were you thinking of?' is a classic ploy car dealers use to make the sale."

"What do you mean?"

"Car dealers are in business to maximize profit. They negotiate dozens of deals each day, whereas the buyer negotiates one deal every few years. Not only that, by the time you're ready to deal, you're emotionally attached to the car you're negotiating for. So you've got an experienced, hard-nosed dealer pitted against an inexperienced buyer who really, really wants the car. Who do you think is getting the short end of the stick?"

"You make it sound like the dealer was out to gouge me."

"That's a bit strong, but for sure the dealer used every advantage he had to make the deal work in his favor."

Larry thought about this for a bit and realized the dealer probably had taken advantage of him. He remembered the day exactly. All those gorgeous cars on the showroom floor, the rich smell of leather as he sat behind the wheel, the solid chunk of the door as the salesman demonstrated the car's construction quality—it had been intoxicating. He would have signed just about anything once the salesman made it clear they could work something out.

"What about this payment thing?"

Roger sensed the defeat in Larry's question and felt sorry for him. Well, he wasn't the first one to make a bad deal on a car. But it was a pity the lesson had to be so expensive.

"The payment game works this way. Any loan has four components: the amount lent, the interest rate, the time over which it is to be repaid, and the monthly payment. Modify any one of those components and the others must change accordingly. For example, assuming the loan amount and the interest rate are fixed, then you can lower the payment by extending the duration of the loan."

"That's why my loan is five years instead of four," said Larry in a flash of understanding. "They dropped my monthly payment but stretched it out a year to earn more interest. Those guys are pretty sneaky!"

"That's probably right," agreed Roger. "And every time the salesman went back to talk with the manager, they were punching numbers into the financial calculator to make sure the sale would still meet their profit target."

"That's what they do in that back room?"

"Actually, only every other time. Half those visits to the manager were just to let you stew a while and get more anxious about closing the deal."

"You're kidding!" said Larry.

"Not at all. Delay is a classic tactic for making the buyer want to finish the negotiation process."

Full realization set in. "They played me pretty good, didn't they?" asked Larry glumly.

"Don't take it too hard. You're wiser now and will do a much better job the next time," assured Roger.

"I sure hope so."

Roger didn't want to kick Larry when he was down, but no sense in leaving the lesson half finished. "They used another classic tactic on you as well. Can you think of what it is?"

Larry mulled this over but couldn't think of anything. Could it really be he had been doubly hoodwinked? The BMW he had once been so eager to own was turning out to be an embarrassment. "No, I don't see it," he said at last.

"I call it the 'diversion' tactic. While you were negotiating on payments, you completely overlooked the total purchase price. That's where the negotiation should have started. In fact, unless you paid cash, every thousand dollars you knock off the purchase price saves you around $1,250 in the long run."

"What, you're telling me a thousand dollars is really worth $1,250? I don't get it."

"Simple math. And I'll bet you can figure it out yourself."

Not another mental math problem. "We'll see," grumbled Larry.

"This is child's play," enthused Roger. "We'll pick real easy numbers to work with."

"I'll bet."

"Here's the question. How much interest will you pay on a $1,000, four-year loan at 10% interest?"

Larry struggled with this one for a while and made little progress. "I can't do compound interest in my head—it's impossible," he whined.

"We're in agreement there. So what's the alternative?"

"Simplify the problem?"

"Exactly. Let's assume that we pay down the same amount of principal each year. What's the loan balance at the start?"

Finally something straightforward. "At the start of the first year, we obviously have the full loan amount of $1,000."

"Good. And at 10%, how much interest will we pay that year?"

"Easy. Ten percent of $1,000 is $100."

"Now you're rolling! File that $100 interest payment away in your memory banks. Now what's the loan balance at the start of the second year?"

"Well, you said we're paying down the same amount of principal each year. So a $1,000 loan over four years means we're paying down $250 per year. So at the start of the second year, the loan balance is down to $750."

"Uh huh. And what interest do we pay in the second year?"

"Well, 10% of the $750 balance is $75."

"Excellent! Add that to the interest paid in the first year and what have you got?"

"That's easy. The $100 from the first year and the $75 from the second year totals $175."

"I think you've got the hang of it. Now walk me through it for the last two years of the loan," instructed Roger.

"OK, after the second year we have $500 remaining on the loan. Ten percent of that is $50, added to the $175 from the first two years comes to $225 interest paid."

"Good—and the last year?"

"Let's see. After the third year we have a loan balance of only $250. Ten percent of that is $25, added to the $225 from before gives us $250 in interest paid over the entire life of the loan."

"Tada! I told you this was child's play. As it turns out, $250 is a bit high since in a real loan you pay interest monthly, which means the outstanding balance shrinks monthly as well. But it's good enough to get a feel for the numbers."

"A feel for the numbers?" huffed Larry. "All that mental math made me forget what we were even talking about."

"Here's the deal," explained Roger patiently. "Most car loans are for four years. So our little exercise showed that if you are paying for the car with a loan, then every $1,000 added to the purchase price actually represents an additional $1,250 that you must pay over time."

"Yeah! And if you look at it the other way, every $1,000 you knock off the purchase price really saves you $1,250 in the long run."

"Exactly! Not to put too fine a point on it then, but you lost twice in your car deal. First you signed up for additional interest by failing to negotiate the purchase price. And then you signed up for even more interest by taking a five-year loan."

"They saw me coming, huh?"

"Fresh meat, my boy. Fresh meat!"

Larry's mind drifted back to his car loan. How much was he overpaying every month because of his inexperience at the negotiating table? Over the life of the loan it had to be several thousand dollars. Big money! It was easily equal to several rent checks or the cost of a deluxe week in Hawaii. Ah, Hawaii. Paradise only a plane ride away. Beaches, surfing...

A dreamy expression betrayed Larry's thoughts. "Are you thinking about what you'd do if you weren't wasting so much on car payments?" asked Roger.

How did he know that? "Yeah, I was dreaming about a trip to Hawaii."

"I love Hawaii. My wife and I go at least once a year to visit my parents."

"Lucky you," replied Larry glumly.

"You could too if you changed some of your habits—cars and other big-ticket items especially."

"How's that?"

"Pay cash!"

"Pay cash? No one pays cash for cars."

"You'd be surprised. It's just that you don't hear about it much. People with enough discipline to save before they buy typically don't brag about it. And dealers don't mention it because they would lose interest income—aside from the fact that Joe Average typically isn't disciplined enough to do it to begin with."

That made sense, but who had that much cash lying around? "I don't see it," said Larry. "Unless you're willing to settle for some el-cheapo tin can."

"You're thinking buying instead of saving," chided Roger.

"What do you mean?"

"Consider your car loan, for example. How long will it take for you to pay it off?"

"Five years."

"That's the key right there—five years. Do you see it yet?"

"See what?"

Roger was surprised Larry didn't get it. "OK, let me phrase it differently. How many years does it take for you to amass the purchase price of the car?"

"Five years—same as before."

"Yes. Do you see it now?"

Larry had a glimmer of comprehension. "I think I get it. You're saying that it takes five years to accumulate the money for a car—regardless of whether you're going to pay cash up front or pay off a loan after."

"That's right. Only there are a couple of key differences." Ever the instructor, Roger asked, "Can you identify them?"

"Well, you'd obviously need the discipline to do the saving if you want to go the 'pay cash' route."

"So true, and often a big stumbling block. But there's another big difference which might help you with that discipline. Any idea what it is?"

After some consideration, Larry mused, "Well, in the save first, pay cash plan, I wouldn't have to pay any interest on a loan."

"Bingo!" approved Roger. "As we calculated earlier, interest payments could be thousands of dollars. But interest plays another role here as well—do you know what it is?"

"Sure!" exclaimed Larry, seeing where this was headed. "In theory the money you are saving is earning interest of its own, thereby reducing the amount you have to save."

"You're on a roll now! Think of loan interest as 'bad interest' and savings interest as 'good interest.' The person buying a car with a loan has zero good interest and all bad interest. The cash buyer on the other hand has all good interest and zero bad interest. Which do you want to be?"

"It's obvious when you spell it out like that," said Larry, "but that discipline thing is still a problem. And what do I do for transportation in the first five years while I'm saving?"

"Those first few years are the hardest part," warned Roger, "but it can be done. Best of all would be to avoid owning a car altogether."

"You're joking—no car at all?"

"I know, it only makes sense if you live and work in a city with good public transportation options. But millions of people in New York, Chicago, and even here in Portland do exactly that."

"And if I don't live in a city?"

"If you just can't exist without a car, then buy the absolute minimum which will fulfill your transportation needs until you have saved enough to enter the 'buy for cash' ranks."

"So no BMW, huh?"

"Be honest," chided Roger. "A BMW of any stripe is a want, not a need."

"What I need," said Larry, hoping to end things swiftly, "is to get to work."

Credit Ratings

It was Roger's turn to pick their meeting spot and he had chosen Heart and Coffee Roasting on the east side of town. Larry would no doubt drive, but at only 20 blocks east of downtown, Roger walked. Portland was a city of bridges and it was always a treat to take in the view, midspan, when crossing the Willamette River. Heart and Coffee advertised siphon brewing, which Roger had never experienced. The method was popular until the 1960s, fell into disuse, but had seen a renaissance among coffee geeks in recent years. In addition to making a tasty drink, siphon brewing was a visual and aural treat with expanding gasses pushing liquid up a tube followed by contracting gasses sucking the brewed mixture through a filter.

Roger debated what the finance topic of the day should be. Larry wanted to know how to make money, so investing might capture his interest. But investing could never make up for ruinous habits, so it seemed premature to dive into stocks and bonds and such. That's why so many lottery winners were broke within a few years of their windfall. They didn't have the financial knowledge and good habits that made holding on to what they'd won possible. Though Larry might be starting to right his listing financial ship, for now he was still a heavy consumer of credit. That might be a place to start.

"Did you know that some people are charged higher interest rates than others on their credit card balances, car loans, and mortgages?" asked Roger.

"That sounds un-American!" said Larry.

"Depends on how you look at it. Maximizing profit is very capitalistic and what could be more American than that?"

"But what about 'all men are created equal'?"

"They may be created equal but they aren't equal credit risks. Guys like you who miss payments are a bigger risk than someone who pays on time every month."

"I guess so," begrudged Larry.

"The difference can really add up. A jump in interest from 7% to 8% on a $250,000 mortgage comes out to $60,000 over the life of the loan."

"Wow, you mean I might have to pay $60,000 more for my house than the next guy just because of bad credit?"

"That's the reality of it—makes you want to improve your credit rating, doesn't it?"

Larry wondered about his car loan and whether he had been stuck with a bad interest rate. How could the dealer have known that his credit cards were maxed out and that he missed payments now and then?

"So what's this credit rating thing?" asked Larry.

"Some people consider it the great conspiracy theory of the computer age."

"What?"

"OK," laughed Roger, "here's how it works. You're aware that many financial transactions are computerized and recorded in a database somewhere, right?"

"Sure."

"Well, there's a handful of companies which gather all that information about you on a monthly basis, analyze it using a formula, and come up with a number between 350 and 850 which is called your credit rating."

"You mean someone is snooping every time I use my debit card or pay a bill? That IS a conspiracy," complained Larry.

"It's not quite that bad. Financial institutions send the credit rating companies summaries on a regular basis. Your every move may not be known, but a good overall picture of your financial habits is maintained."

"What if I don't want to be spied on like that?" asked Larry.

"About the only way to escape scrutiny would be to buy everything with cash—in which case you wouldn't ever need to apply for credit, would you? But that's not really possible for most people."

"Right," acknowledged Larry. "So how can I find out my rating?"

"That's easy," replied Roger. "There are three main companies which provide credit ratings—Experian, TransUnion, and Equifax. Each is required by law to give you a peek into their file on you once a year. You can request it over the internet."

"That sounds easy enough. Will the report include my credit rating?"

"Unfortunately not. They are only required to tell you what they know about you, not what number their formula assigns to you. But the exact number isn't all that interesting anyway."

"But I thought my credit rating determined how much I'll pay in interest," said Larry.

"You've been paying attention. Very good. The problem is that institutions which make loans often have their own formula to determine what kind of risk you are. Car companies have their favorite formula, mortgage brokers have another, and so on. But almost all of them use the data from your aggregated file as input to their formula."

"So why should I bother to check my file if it doesn't tell me what I want to know?"

"Good question—why do you think?" countered Roger.

Larry didn't like his question being turned back on him. The whole idea was for Roger to spill the beans, not for him to do any hard thinking. But it didn't sound like Roger was going to volunteer any more information.

"Try thinking out loud," suggested Roger.

"Well," began Larry, "asking for my reports would at least let me see what others know about me. I guess that's useful."

"That's right. And if you know what data are considered good or bad, then you'll have an idea of how a credit granting organization might think of you."

"Like what?" asked Larry.

"Good data should be obvious—low balances on credit cards and no history of late payments."

"That's it?"

"Then there's the red flags—too many credit cards, cards held for only a short period of time, frequent credit checks which might indicate an unhealthy appetite for debt, and that sort of thing."

"What are credit checks?"

"That's when someone other than yourself takes a look at your file. Typically it's someone with whom you are applying for a loan––though it could also be a prospective employer, or really anyone willing to pay for it."

"What! You mean a company can check out my financial history as part of the interview process?"

"Sure, and it's done more than you realize. Who do you think they want handling their money—someone who is debt free and handles money wisely in their own life, or the slacker who is in debt up to their ears?"

"Well, if you put it that way..." said Larry.

Larry considered when someone may have performed a check on him. "So did the car dealer do a credit check on me too?"

"Most definitely. It's the first thing they did once they realized you were a real prospect. Otherwise they wouldn't know what interest rate to offer you."

"No way. They didn't even know who I was until we started doing the paperwork at the end," claimed Larry.

"They asked for a copy of your driver's license before you could go for a test drive, right?"

"Yeah."

"And what do you think the office manager was doing while you and the sales guy were driving around the neighborhood?"

"They were checking me out?"

"They had your financial profile down to the last late fee by the time you drove back onto the lot. You didn't have a chance."

"What a racket!"

"No racket, just business as usual."

Larry was disturbed by the knowledge that his financial habits were being recorded and available to such a wide variety of people. Maybe the current system WAS the conspiracy of the computer age.

"How did it work before the days of computers and electronic commerce?" wondered Larry.

"Good question. There were two main differences. The first is that credit just wasn't as available as it is now."

"You mean no credit cards?"

"That's right. Much of society worked strictly with cash except for the one big purchase of their life, their house. And there, bankers required down payments of 20% or more, which tended to weed out those who didn't know how to manage their money."

"People bought their wide-screen TVs for cash?" asked an incredulous Larry.

"We're talking the 1960s and earlier, so there weren't any wide-screen TVs yet. But yes, larger items were typically bought for cash or on layaway," said Roger.

"And the second difference?"

"Rather than some faceless computer deciding your credit worthiness based on data and statistical averages, your local banker made the call."

"Like Mr. Drysdale in *The Beverly Hillbillies*?"

"Exactly—and I'm glad to hear you're a fan of classic TV. Should we sing the theme song?"

"No thanks," said Larry, thinking Roger was turning a bit weird on him.

"Fine," said Roger, sounding disappointed. "Nowadays, you'll only deal with a real person if you are borrowing a big enough amount."

"How do you mean?"

"Consider someone like Donald Trump. When he wants to borrow mega-millions to develop a property, they don't just plug the numbers into a computer and out pops his interest rate. Instead, it's a negotiated deal with lots of haggling back and forth on how to assess the risk and set the terms of the loan."

"So you're saying that until I start throwing around the millions, I won't have a personal relationship with my banker?"

"Probably so," said Roger. "And that's why maintaining a good credit rating is so important. Your cost of credit will be determined by your credit rating, which in turn is determined by your financial habits. Use credit sparingly and pay on time to save big in the long run."

"You always put it back on me," sighed Larry.

"That's reality for you," grinned Roger.

Statistics showed that most people didn't check their files once a year at the three credit report companies. Many people were turned off by offers to look up their report for a fee. As long as credit kept getting approved, why pay extra for something that wasn't a problem? Alternatively, one could request the free annual report as mandated by law. But the web sites to do this were tedious and tried to up-sell other credit services every step of the way. Only the highly motivated ended up getting their three free reports annually. What might give Larry this motivation?

"Larry, how hard would it be for me to get your mom's maiden name?"

"That's easy, just ask your brother!"

"What I meant was, how hard would it be for any random individual to uncover your mother's maiden name?" asked Roger.

Larry had done his share of snooping on the internet and understood the power of search engines. "A net-savvy kid could probably find it within five minutes."

"Now how about your social security number?" continued Roger.

"That might be a bit tougher, but I suppose it's out there as well."

"It sure is. Consider how many institutions use your SSN as the key for your data—the government, doctors, banks, schools, and utilities."

"But aren't those all supposed to be confidential?"

"They're supposed to be. But data are only as confidential as the least trustworthy person who has access. And given the number of passwords I've seen on sticky notes plastered to computer monitors, even the cleaning crew has access to your data if they want it."

"You see a crook under every rock," charged an idealistic Larry.

"And you're naïve if you think your social security number isn't already floating around the internet somewhere."

"So what's your point?" asked Larry.

"Your name, address, and social security number are all that's required for you to be the victim of identity theft."

"How does that work exactly?"

"There are many forms of identity theft, but the simplest is to apply for credit using someone else's identity. Your credit rating is used to approve the purchase, the crook gets the stuff, and you're left with the bill."

"It can't be that easy, can it?"

"At over 10 million cases per year in the U.S. alone, it must be easy," said Roger. "But there's a simple way to protect yourself."

"Don't have any credit cards?"

"That will eliminate some forms of identity theft, but even those without credit cards have a credit file at the three rating companies."

Larry was stumped. If everyone had a credit file and no one could effectively hide their social security number, then how could you protect yourself?

"The secret is to ask each of the credit rating companies to put a credit freeze on your file," revealed Roger. "Once frozen, all credit checks are refused and though a crook may have your data, it does him no good."

"What's the sense in that? Then I can't even use my own credit cards," complained Larry.

"Not true. You can use the cards you have all you want. You just can't apply for new cards or new loans without temporarily lifting the freeze."

"Why can't the crook lift my freeze if he's got all my information?" asked Larry.

"Only you can do that with the secret PIN you were given when you froze the file."

"I get it now. The PIN lets me unfreeze the file only when I want someone to check my credit. Everyone else is locked out."

"Exactly. And there's a second benefit as well," teased Roger. "Can you figure it out?"

It wasn't obvious so Larry thought about it while taking the final sip of his latte. His only real credit experience had been buying the BMW and that hadn't exactly been planned. He had gone for the test drive on a whim and ended up buying that day because the car was so sweet and they were able to work out a deal. Then the insight hit him. That impulse purchase wouldn't have been possible with a credit freeze.

"I've got it," announced Larry. "The credit freeze prohibits impulse purchases which require a credit check. It forces you to plan ahead."

"You get an A+ for today," lauded Roger. "I do believe you're starting to see the light."

Emergency Fund

Portland summers more than made up for any of its other weather deficiencies. Each day dawned crystal clear and stayed that way until late in the afternoon when a few puffy clouds rolled in. Those were usually gone by nightfall again, making for scenic sunsets and starlit nights. Daytime temperatures rarely rose above eighty degrees—warm enough for women to show off their summer ensembles, but without anyone suffering heatstroke. Locals took pride in noting that while most of the country was bright red on the national weather map, the Pacific Northwest stayed a relatively cool yellow. And what passed for humidity here was a crisp fall day anywhere else.

Alas, fall was coming and cloudy days were starting to outnumber sunny ones. Water Avenue Coffee in the southeast industrial district was the perfect antidote to a cloudy day. Large windows let in plenty of light which reflected warmly off pastel walls and natural wood. The shop provided a human element of warmth as well. Unlike many coffee shops where the barista was hidden behind a wheezing machine while customers waited in a herd, Water Avenue featured a pour-over coffee bar. Experts created your single-cup concoction directly across from you, engaging you in conversation while you watched them transform beans to elixir. Roger had picked this spot, figuring it was time to broaden Larry's coffee horizons.

"So Larry, ever been bungee jumping?" asked Roger.

"Naw, that's a little crazy for me. I've got an issue with heights."

"Me too. I haven't been to the edge of the balcony in years. Love the view, but standing near the edge gives me the willies."

"Same here."

"Yet I'll bet you're on the edge right now."

"What?"

"I mean financially. My guess is that if you don't get your next paycheck, you won't be able to make rent this month."

"So?" replied Larry, turning sullen.

"Let's say your company has a cash crunch and asks you to take two weeks off without pay. Or you need a new transmission. Or you chip a tooth and that isn't covered by your health plan. Or whatever. What are you going to do?"

"Isn't that what credit cards are for?" shrugged Larry.

"I'm not sure you can pay rent with a credit card. Even if you could, how do you then pay the credit card if you're already living hand to mouth? One blip in your life and you're in a debt spiral of death."

Larry had no answer to that. In fact, he was there already— juggling credit cards and paying minimums only. He'd be in serious trouble if he got hit with a big repair bill or something. And it would be a total disaster to miss a paycheck.

"You could always move back in with Mom and Dad," suggested Roger. "The food might be better, but if you think getting dates is difficult now…"

"I get it already," muttered Larry.

"What you need is an emergency fund. Something to help you through the unexpected rough spots."

"An emergency fund?"

"A pool of money that's always there in case of an emergency. And by emergency, I don't mean running out of Twizzlers or not having the latest gadget. Emergencies are things like loss of income, unplanned medical expenses, unexpected car repairs, that sort of thing."

"How big does this emergency fund need to be? I mean, how do I know what's going to break next on my car?"

"Good question. One way to plan it is by time. How many months do you want to be able to survive without income at your current standard of living—same apartment, same car, same monthly payments, etc.?"

"That's crazy. I'd need thousands of dollars to cover even one month. Besides, I'm not losing my job anytime soon."

So young, naïve, and with no knowledge of history, thought Roger. "You'd be surprised how quickly things can change. Your company could lose its biggest customer to a competitor. The accountant could be embezzling funds. The overall economy could fizzle. Your boss might replace you in favor of his new son-in-law. Things happen."

"No way! My company has been doing great for years."

"And what are you personally doing to guarantee it stays that way? You don't need to be a pessimist, just a realist. Much of life is out of your control and the emergency fund helps you ride through the rough spots."

"I just don't see any of that happening to me. Everything is going great."

"I can see that you're an optimist. That's nice. But to a certain extent, belief in the need for an emergency fund is a matter of faith."

"You're not getting mystical on me, are you?"

"Nothing like that. It's much simpler. Either you believe that bad things are possible and out of your control or you don't. Those that believe have the incentive to be prepared. Those that don't are trusting to luck."

"Guess I'm one of the lucky ones then!"

So far. Being optimistic was commendable, but this was plain ignoring reality. Roger knew that despite a regular salary, his nephew was living paycheck to paycheck, was in debt up to his eyeballs, and didn't have two nickels to rub together. He'd give it one more try, frustrating as it may be.

"I'm no fan of sensationalist news reporting," began Roger, "but the media's coverage of layoffs, accidents, illnesses, mudslides – you name it – proves that such things do happen. Do you honestly believe you're so special you'll never experience one of life's misfortunes?"

"I suppose something like that could happen."

Maybe there was hope yet. "Statistically speaking, you're not that special. None of us are."

"You're crushing my self-esteem!" joked Larry.

"All right. You are special. But even so, things happen. Best to be prepared and have a little something stashed away."

"A couple months' worth, you say?"

"It sounds like a lot, but look at the worst-case scenario. How long would it take to find another job to replace your current income?"

"I don't know."

"And during that time, you'd want to maintain your current standard of living. That's hardly the time to move or have to give up your vehicle."

"My business goes in cycles. When things are slow, it might be months until people start hiring again."

"Now you're thinking."

"But several months of living expenses is huge. That would take forever to build up."

"But it's what you should do before anything else—before making big purchases, taking on debt, or adding to your fixed expenses."

"No wonder no one does it."

"Sad but true. Most people do exactly the wrong thing once they start earning some real money. Instead of using their newfound income to become financially stable, they actually do their best to become financially unstable."

"I suppose that's me, huh?" asked Larry.

"Uh huh. You're a classic example. You maximized your fixed expenses with a high rent, spent to your credit limit, and took on a hefty car loan. Now you're in a box. Granted, it's one of your own making, but a box nonetheless."

"How am I in a box?"

"Isn't it obvious? You have no freedom," said Roger.

"That's not true!" objected Larry. "I've got as much freedom as the next guy."

"No, you have as little freedom as the next guy. There's a big difference."

"You're talking in circles."

"Look. If you wanted to take a year off sailing to Tahiti, could you?"

"No."

"If you decided to become a street musician could you?"

"No."

"If you became disenchanted with architecture and wanted to go back to school to study to become a chiropractor, could you?"

"No, but then I don't want to be a chiropractor."

"If you had a great idea for a killer product, could you go off and start a company?"

"No."

"And why is that?" asked Roger.

Larry was slowly getting it. "Well, I've got bills. They need to be paid."

"That's right. Your financial obligations have you strapped in like a straitjacket. Financial freedom and personal freedom go hand in hand. You're about as unfree as one can get financially, therefore you also have no personal freedom."

"What, so I have to be poor to be free?"

"No, to be free you have to live beneath your means and have an adequate emergency fund. Freedom isn't about dollar amounts. Freedom is whether you have choices."

Larry was starting to regret having agreed to keep meeting with Roger. On the surface he was a nice enough guy and seemed to know something about finance. But all he did was make Larry feel foolish about his choices in life. Who cared if it was all true—couldn't the guy say something nice now and then?

A long stretch of silence had Roger wondering whether he had offended his pupil. No one liked bad news, no matter how accurate it might be. He hadn't been all that brilliant during his youth himself. Many of his choices in life had turned out to be lucky, not wise, so he didn't really have much moral high ground to stand on. How would he have responded to some older guy telling him how stupid he was: not very kindly, that's for sure!

"Sorry about all that freedom stuff," offered Roger. "That's a pet topic of mine and I got a bit carried away. You've been working hard and seem like a guy who does better when he knows better, so take pride in that."

"Thanks," said Larry, wondering where this sudden contrition was coming from.

"But..." began Roger.

"I know. There's still the emergency fund, right?"

"Yup."

"I get the why, but I don't see the how. Everything is so tight already."

"You've got to give up something, that's for sure," said Roger. "Rome wasn't built in a day. You can build up to it a bit at a time. Eat out a few less times a week and put the money you save in a safe place instead."

"Like my mattress?"

"If you want. You could put your change in a bowl every night and deposit it in the bank every Saturday."

"Or I could hide it in my sock drawer."

"That too. Another way to build up some savings is to pay yourself first."

"Pay myself? I don't get it."

"Paying yourself first is a simple psychological trick that seems to work for lots of people."

"I'm going to psych myself out once a week?" asked Larry.

"Not really. Whenever you get some money, like a paycheck, you immediately transfer some amount, either a dollar value or a percentage, to your emergency fund."

"Sounds simple enough, but where's the psychological trick?"

"People always seem to be able to squeeze by with whatever amount of money they have left. So the trick is that you skim money off the top for a good cause, knowing that somehow you'll make do with what's left."

"I don't know, sounds kinda stupid to me."

"Stupid but effective."

"Like the mattress idea, huh?"

"Well, by a safe place I meant a savings vehicle where maintenance of principal is guaranteed and you have immediate access."

"Like a savings account?"

"That would be good. Your principal is guaranteed by FDIC insurance and you can withdraw the money at any time. Insured certificates of deposit are fine as well."

"What about other investments, like stocks or something."

"The big problem there is that your stock may be down right when you need the money. So you want something as close to a cash equivalent as possible. This isn't your long-term investment nest egg which fluctuates with market conditions, it's your emergency fund. One hundred percent secure and highly available is what you want."

"Boring and big enough, that's the perfect emergency fund?"

"Exactly."

Both were briefly sidetracked watching the drink being made a few seats away. A laundry list of additional ingredients made one wonder if it would taste like coffee at all in the end. Given the number of detailed instructions given by the customer, they were a real connoisseur or liked to hear themselves talk. Maintaining their professional demeanor, the barista made the beverage as requested without a misstep.

Roger knew that while building an adequate emergency fund was critical to financial security, it was a monumental stumbling block for most. It went against human nature in so many ways. First, you were going without today for an unknown need tomorrow. How were you supposed to get worked up over something that wasn't even defined? Second, the money you set aside had to be in something 100% safe, which meant it likely wouldn't grow much, if at all. Who would like sitting on money you weren't allowed to spend but that also wasn't working for you?

"So how many months of emergency fund would you like to put aside?" asked Roger, assuming Larry was already committed to the idea.

"How about I start with one?"

"Not enough, but certainly a meaningful start. How are you going to do it?"

"Do that pay-yourself-first plan somehow?" fished Larry.

"Good idea, but how exactly?" probed Roger.

"I could transfer a couple bucks to my savings account every time I deposit a paycheck."

"Or you could set up a recurring electronic transfer."

"Some guys get paid that way."

"This is the same kind of thing, only the transfer is from your checking account to your savings account. Now building up your emergency fund requires no intervention on your part, it just happens."

"Except I better deposit my paychecks on time."

"When's the last time that didn't happen?"

Insurance

Walking down Broadway, Roger debated the wisdom of picking a place he had never been to. That was like a lawyer asking a witness a question he didn't already know the answer to. You might get a nasty surprise. But from the reports he had read, while Courier Coffee Roasters might not have the greatest ambience, their brew was superb and absolutely fresh. Every drink was fresh made, not pulled from a heated urn of questionable age. The firm originally roasted small batches daily and delivered them by bicycle to coffee shops around town—hence the name. The retail shop opened last summer and seemed to be a success.

Despite their regular get-togethers, Larry typically didn't give money matters another thought until Roger's electronic reminder the night before their next meeting. This week had been different though. The day after their last meeting was payday, so Roger's advice was fresh in his mind when he went to deposit his paycheck. Deviating from habit, he bypassed the ATM and went inside to set up a biweekly transfer to his savings account. Now he couldn't wait to impress Roger with his financial progress. Sliding into the seat across from Roger, he skipped the usual pleasantries and triumphantly announced, "Eight months!"

Roger had never seen his tutee so animated, at least not this early in the morning. "Eight months?" he echoed.

"That's when I'll have the first month of my emergency fund in place!"

"So you're paying yourself first?"

"You bet. Twice a month, a couple of days after payday."

"Congratulations! But how do you figure the eight months?"

Larry was real proud of this part. "First I figured out my after-tax income since that's what I really spend."

"Except when you're adding to your credit card balances," noted Roger. "But your reasoning is sound."

Larry could hardly contain himself. Here was the perfect opportunity to hit Roger with some of his own mental math medicine.

"So what's that come out to?"

"Easy," replied Roger, seeing no reason to spoil Larry's fun. "Let's see, assuming a 20% tax rate and that you spend everything left over, then your after-tax expenses are 80% of $25,000 or $20,000."

"Good. Now how much is that each month?" asked Larry, thinking division by 12 would stump his uncle.

"Well, I can't give it to you exactly since division by twelve can get sort of ugly."

"Aha!"

"Keep your shirt on. We can do it a different way and get very close."

"Oh yeah?" taunted Larry.

"Let's round down the number of weeks in a year from 52 to 50. Then the $20,000 per year divided by 50 weeks comes to $400 per week. Multiply by approximately 4 weeks per month gives $1,600 per month. That should be pretty close to the real number."

Larry allowed that it was awfully close to the monthly expenses of $1,666 he had obtained with a calculator. "Not bad."

"And if you're saving that over an eight-month period, that comes to $200 a month or $100 transferred after each biweekly paycheck. Am I on the mark?" asked Roger.

Larry reviewed what he'd learned so far. Drop the mindless spending habits. Check. Put together a financial plan. Check. Buy smart. Check. Create an emergency fund. Check. Maybe they could finally start talking about how to make his money grow. After all, once the emergency fund was in place, he'd have $200 per month to invest.

"Can we talk about investing now?" asked Larry anxiously.

"Sorry, but the emergency fund is only the first step in being prepared for life's uncertainties."

"You mean we have to do something else first? What?"

"Insurance."

"I thought that's what the emergency fund is."

"Sort of. The emergency fund is a form of self-insurance to help you through a rough spot without having to radically change your standard of living or sell things at an inopportune time. But it isn't enough to handle bigger or longer-term problems."

"Such as?"

"Major medical procedures, accident damages, property loss, income loss due to disability, lawsuits, financial obligations after your death—that sort of thing."

"You're a regular doomsday machine," complained Larry.

"Just being a realist."

"I've got medical insurance through work and insurance on my car, isn't that enough?"

"It depends. You'd be surprised how people end up with too much of an insurance they don't need and too little of the one they do. For example, lots of young folks have way too much life insurance but almost no disability insurance. It should be the other way around."

"What do I need disability insurance for? It's not as though I'm going to hurt myself punching numbers into a calculator."

"True enough. Who ever heard of 'calculator finger'? But you're making a common mistake in how you are thinking about insurance."

"I am?"

"Insurance isn't about the probability of something occurring. It's for dealing with the consequence of something occurring. What would happen if you couldn't work because of an injury—whether it occurred at work or not? Imagine something serious requiring months of rehabilitation."

Larry replayed the near misses of his life. He had a permanent neck tweak from an off-road motorcycling spill a few years ago. Much faster and that might have been a serious injury. Then there was the back problem after helping a friend move into a new house. He'd been flat on his back for days. It was that third U-haul load that did him in. He had been fine up till then. And just this past season he was beaned during a softball game. He'd been woozy for a long time after that one. You never knew what could happen with head injuries.

"I see what you mean. One bad day and you can't work for months."

"Yet most people have only minimal short-term disability insurance and even less long-term disability insurance."

"Is it expensive?" asked Larry.

"Not compared to the alternative. Just about everything you have, enjoy, or do is only possible because you have a steady income. Lose that and where are you?"

Larry was confused about what was actually being insured and ventured, "So disability insurance insures against loss of income?"

"Exactly. It's misnamed, in a way. Think of it as insuring the continuation of your income in case it is disrupted by a disability."

"What about life insurance?" asked Larry.

"What about it?"

"This agent has been trying to sell me something he calls 'whole life.' Is that something I really need?"

"It's the form of insurance that pays the agent the highest commission, so I doubt it."

"No wonder he's bugging me so much. But I do need life insurance, right?"

"It depends. Once you get past all the fluff, life insurance primarily exists to provide a pot of money upon your death. So what's the consequence, the financial consequence that is, of your death?"

"I don't know."

"You've got debts, right? Do you want them to be paid off?"

"I suppose."

"And it costs a few bucks to be cremated or buried."

"OK."

"So how much money would be required to clean the slate if you died?"

"If I include what I owe on the car, my credit card balances, and the student loan, I'd guess it's around $40,000."

"That sounds reasonable. And I wouldn't be surprised if that's part of your employee benefits package already."

"Yes, it is! In fact, the payout is $50,000."

"Then I'd say you don't need any additional life insurance."

"But this salesman keeps telling me I need a whole life policy with a death benefit of one million dollars. Is he snowing me?"

Roger wasn't a fan of insurance agents and their tactics. But he didn't want to come across as too critical. The problem was one of education. People starting out in their careers were woefully uneducated on their insurance needs and thus easy pickings for pushy salesmen.

"Once you understand your life insurance needs, you can decide for yourself whether that sales guy is conning you."

"I'd say he is since he wants to sell me a million-dollar policy when I only need one for $40,000."

"Today, maybe."

"What do you mean? If I start saving and getting out of debt, then I'll need even less life insurance, not more."

"That's true. And it cheers me to hear you talk about saving. But imagine yourself, say, ten years from now. You're married, have a mortgage, and 1.8 kids as per the national average. I'd say the financial consequence of an early death has changed dramatically, wouldn't you?"

"Now you can tell the future too? Did I marry a blonde?" joked Larry.

"I don't know about the blonde. But consider your future situation. In the event of your death, should the house get paid off? Should your wife have to work or should the life insurance provide her with an annual income? What about college education for your kids? Are they out of luck now that you, um, exited so early? And don't forget any consumer debt you might have at the time."

"Wow, that's a whole lot of stuff. It would cost a fortune to cover all that."

"Yes it would. Your insurance guy can help you put an exact number on it, but it could easily top a million dollars."

"A million dollars, where do you get that?"

"Well, we could try to add up all the things I listed earlier—the mortgage, income for your wife, college educations, etc. But there's a much simpler way to look at it. Remember the lifetime earnings calculation we made earlier?"

"Sure, it came out to about two million dollars."

"Let's assume that you died midlife and given that you were married with kids at the time, the second half of your life's earnings was mostly intended for your family. Well, that's a million right there."

"If you want to look at it that way."

"I can see you're not in a committed relationship yet," laughed Roger. "That scenario was just to illustrate the point, but you have to acknowledge it as a possibility."

"I guess so," said Larry, though the idea of settling down was, well, unsettling to say the least.

Roger wondered whether Larry's agent ever explained the difference between term insurance and whole life. How typical for the agent to push Larry toward the more expensive, higher commission product right from the start. Not only did a whole life policy cost more, but it was much harder to get out of as well.

"Did your agent ever tell you about alternatives to a whole life policy?"

"No, not really. He just said that was best for me in the long run."

"Didn't that make you suspicious?"

"Nope. What do I know about insurance?"

"Exactly. Since you know you don't know, then alarm bells should start ringing when an expert tries to sell you something. There are always choices, you just have to find them and understand them."

"Boy, you really don't like insurance salesmen, do you?"

"It's not them in particular. A salesperson, whatever the product, is just doing their job. But you should never forget that what's in their best interest is not what's in your best interest. They want to maximize their profit which, unfortunately, has to come out of your pocket."

"Buyer beware, huh?"

"Absolutely—whether you're buying cars, insurance, investments, or anything else. Take that to heart and you'll do fine."

Larry realized they had gotten off track due to Roger's salesman issues. "What's so bad about whole life insurance and what's the alternative?"

"No two policies are identical, so you need to read the fine print. But generally a whole life policy covers you for your entire life and has some kind of forced savings or investment component. Often you can borrow against the accrued savings, though that would then reduce the death benefit."

"OK, and term?"

"Term insurance is real simple. It pays a known amount upon your death for the term of the policy, typically one year. You can think of it as pure insurance with no investment bells or whistles. You buy exactly as much coverage as you need when you need it— no more and no less."

"That does sound simple. But do I have to buy it every year for the rest of my life? That doesn't sound all that different from the whole life version."

"Not necessarily. It depends on your plan."

"My plan?"

"Sure. Let's fast forward to when you're, say, 60 years old and assume you never got on track financially. You haven't saved for retirement, you've been remortgaging your house regularly for the cash, and you used loans to send your kids to college. What's your family left with if you die?"

"Lots of debt?"

"Exactly. So in that scenario, you better have some life insurance to help pay things off—and extra money for your dependents to live on."

"That would be nice of me, I guess."

"You bet. Now let's bring your financially savvy clone back into the picture. He paid off his mortgage a long time ago, buys all his cars for cash, started college savings plans the day each kid was born, and given that he's 60, has adequately funded his retirement by now. Does he need life insurance?"

"Not so much."

"That's right. He's got no debts to pay and his wife can live off the retirement savings. Not only that, every year as he moved closer to this point, he was able to buy less insurance, thereby saving money."

"That darn clone. He's so smart."

"It's the same old story. You can pay it now or you can pay it later. It's just that later it usually costs more. You decide."

"The plan, huh?"

"Uh huh. The plan."

"You know," summarized Larry, "that bit about consequence, not probability, really simplifies figuring out whether you need insurance or not."

"I'm glad to hear that, though you may still be amazed at how many kinds of insurance there are out there. Whatever consequence you can think of, there's an insurance you can buy for it—theft, lawsuit, injury, accident, etc. But there's no insurance for lack of financial education. That's still up to you."

Investing Overview

Larry and Roger were meeting at Caffé D'Arte in the Lloyd Center district east of downtown. It was just before noon and Roger waited at the quietest table he could find. Larry arrived promptly, rolls of engineering drawings clutched in his arms.

"Got to deliver these to a customer after lunch," announced Larry, as he laid the rolls across the seat of a chair.

"And here I assumed you were just trying to get a free meal," heckled Roger.

"You want to help me save or not," came the retort.

"I want to help you think!"

The duo wandered up to the counter to place their orders. Roger selected a salad and sandwich combo. Larry opted for a bagel construction with eggs, bacon, cheese, and mystery sauce plus a bag of chips. Roger dove right into discussion once they were back at their table.

"Let's talk about investing today," opened Roger.

"It's about time," said Larry. "I get that tracking expenses, an emergency fund, adequate insurance, and having a plan are necessary for financial stability. But that's pretty dull stuff."

"I can't promise investing will be all that exciting."

"What? Invest money. Watch it grow. Spend it. That sounds exciting to me, especially the spending part."

"What would you spend your money on if you were lucky enough to invest successfully?"

"How much time do you have?" asked Larry with a grin. "My wish list is pretty long."

"Is saving for retirement on that list?"

"No way! That's too far off to worry about for now."

"Clearly you haven't done the math. I read an article on this recently and the way the numbers work out is fascinating."

Roger must be sick, concluded Larry. "Well, one man's fascinating is another man's booooring. I've probably got 30 or more years until retirement. I don't see what the rush is."

"That's exactly what this article was about," enthused Roger. "It showed how putting aside relatively small amounts of money early in one's career is more effective and less painful than socking away large amounts of money later on."

"Less is more, huh?" kidded Larry.

"Exactly. The article showed that if you put aside $5,000 per year in the first ten years of your career and let it sit the next 30 years earning 5% interest, you would have about $270,000 at retirement."

"That doesn't sound too bad."

"No it doesn't," replied Roger. "But here's the real interesting part. If you put off saving until the last ten years of your career, then you would need to put aside $21,500 per year to build up the same nest egg."

"I thought $5,000 per year was a lot. But $21,500? Every year for ten years? That's insane."

"Yes it is. Now here's the insight. How much money did you have to contribute in the two plans to amass that $270,000 retirement fund?"

Larry didn't like getting hit with these mental math quizzes, but this one was easy since the time period in question was ten years in each case. "In the save early plan, I had to put aside $5,000 for ten years, or $50,000 total. In the save late plan, I had to put aside $21,500 for ten years, or $215,000 total."

"Very good. I'm glad to see you can put a zero on the end of a number without making a mistake," ribbed Roger. "So which makes more sense, putting aside the $50,000 or putting aside the $215,000?"

"That's a no-brainer. Putting aside $50,000 is a lot easier. But only if you've got it to begin with."

"That's true. But look at it this way. Twenty-five or so years from now when you're ten years away from retirement, do you expect to be motivated to save for retirement?"

"Of course. By then it's getting pretty close and with raises and such, I'll have the money to put aside."

"I sincerely doubt that part about having the money later, given your spending habits," chided Roger. "But let's leave that aside for now. So you're saying that 25 years from now, you'll have wised up and be ready to commit to saving for retirement?"

"Sure. The future me is going to be a model citizen!" assured Larry.

"Let's bring back your clone who earns just like you do but spends smarter. Say your clone does the early saving plan while you do the late plan. What's the difference between you and your clone on retirement day?"

At first, all Larry could think of was the absurdity of coming up with $5,000 per year to put into retirement savings. But was that really more absurd than coming up with $21,500 a year later on? Or spending $2,000 a year at Starbucks now? Then the difference between his clone and him became apparent.

"Wow!" exclaimed Larry. "My clone invested only $50,000 during his career while I had to invest $215,000, which means my clone had $165,000 more to spend on stuff than I did!"

"That's right. While you enter retirement driving a beater and not having had a vacation in ten years because you're scrimping to put aside the big bucks, your clone enters retirement driving a top of the line Porsche, paid for no less, and reminiscing about a decade of great vacation trips. Who do you want to be, Larry?"

"You make it sound so easy," whined Larry, "but it isn't. I don't know anyone who puts away $5,000 per year for their retirement. That's nuts."

"Hey, if you want your retirement fund to cost $165,000 more than it has to, that's your decision. Start as late as you want."

"There goes my wish list," lamented Larry.

"Think positive—here comes your comfortable retirement."

Their plates were empty by this time and Roger suggested his partner bus the dishes while he ordered postprandial coffees. There was a line at the counter, so Roger gave his nephew a problem to work on while he waited his turn.

"Think about those retirement numbers from earlier and calculate the multiplier effect," said Roger.

Larry would have asked what a multiplier effect even was, but Roger had already gone up front to place their orders. The only thing that came to mind was the phrase 'double your money.' Put in one dollar, get back two. Well, that calculation could be performed for Roger's retirement savings scenario as well. The guy investing only in the last ten years before retirement ended up with a nest egg 1.3 times as big as what he put in. But smarty pants clone who invested in the first ten years and then just waited for compounding to do its thing ended up with a nest egg 5.4 times as big as what he put in. Investing sure seemed like a race for turtles, not hares.

Roger returned with their drinks and immediately hit Larry with another question.

"Why is it that we don't use the same money strategies for both the emergency and retirement funds?" asked Roger.

Larry's first thought was that this was a trick question. After all, people always talked about 'saving for retirement.' But none of the older guys at work ever talked about their savings accounts. They gabbed about how their investments were doing and whether the market was up or down for the year.

"I don't get it," said Larry. "How can saving be good for an emergency fund yet bad for retirement?"

"Did you know that I paid only 29 cents per gallon for gas in my teens?" asked Roger, seemingly out of the blue.

"You're kidding! It's at least ten times that now."

"Uh huh. And what do we call that phenomenon?"

"Inflation!" answered Larry after a brief contemplation.

"You have now answered why emergency fund-style saving doesn't work for retirement. Do you see it?"

Larry felt it had something to do with the rate of inflation compared to the rate of return on the savings account where the emergency fund was kept, but it wasn't completely clear yet.

"Is it because of interest rates?" he asked hopefully.

"You're on the right track. Let's say your savings account earned 2% per year but inflation was 3% per year. Would your savings account grow each year?"

"Sure—by 2%."

"But would it buy more each year?"

In a flash of insight, Larry realized what would happen. Sure, each $1.00 in the savings account had grown to $1.02 a year later. But all things which cost $1.00 a year ago now cost $1.03 due to inflation. So although the money grew, it bought less.

"I'm saving like I'm supposed to, but still end up with less for my money. What a rip-off," said Larry.

"That's called 'inflation risk.' And like compounding, over a long period of time the effect can be significant. In fact, over the 35 to 40 years you'll be preparing for retirement, it could be devastating. Instead of steak and lobster, you could end up eating beans and rice."

"So what am I supposed to do?"

"That's where investing comes in."

"So investing is where my money grows fast enough to beat inflation?" asked Larry.

"That's the general idea. But there is no free lunch. Since you're trying to do better than an ultra-safe savings account, you're going to have to accept more risk."

"But that means I might lose money too, right?"

"That's the way the money game works. More risk generally means the results are magnified – to your benefit or to your detriment – depending on how things work out."

Larry didn't like this talk of losing money. He knew how hard it was to put money aside. Setting up that automatic transfer for the emergency fund had required enormous resolve. But it irked him that even if he were to do the right thing and start planning for the future, he could actually end up losing money.

"It doesn't seem fair," he complained. "You do the right thing and still could get screwed."

"Who said life is fair?" asked Roger. "Drop that idea and look at the facts. You can be safe but have the buying power of your savings eroded by inflation. Or you can invest with more risk, carefully mind you, and with luck and time possibly come out ahead. Those are your choices."

"You're saying I have to invest just so I don't fall behind?"

"Pretty much," agreed Roger.

"So tell me how to invest," said Larry.

"How much time do you have?" laughed Roger, parroting Larry's own line from earlier. "Libraries are full of books on investing."

"Just give me an overview then."

"All right, but you have to promise me one thing. Educate yourself and never invest in something you don't understand. 'A fool and his money are soon parted' is a popular adage for good reason."

"I promise," said Larry, as he flashed the three-finger Boy Scout salute.

"Good—here we go. Investing is simple in concept but complicated in practice. In principle, there are only two kinds of investing—lending and buying."

"Sounds easy enough, especially the buying part. I'm good at that," joked Larry.

"We'll see. Let's start with lending. The basic premise is straightforward. You lend someone money and they pay you back more."

"Oh yeah, we talked about that earlier—like lending money to the bank. Only that didn't pay much interest."

"Right. But it's not just banks who want to borrow your money. Governments, municipalities, and companies of all kinds and sizes will pay to use your money for a while."

"I can lend my money to a government?"

"Sure. The United States government is one of the biggest debt holders in the world. You can even lend your money to the government of Zimbabwe, though I wouldn't necessarily recommend it."

"Or a company?"

"No problem. Say Coca-Cola wants to build a new bottling plant somewhere before Pepsi does, but doesn't have the cash on hand. In order to take advantage of the business opportunity, they borrow the money from people like you and often pay handsomely for the privilege."

"How does that work? I've never heard of Coca-Cola asking for money."

"We can get into the details later, but that's what the folks on Wall Street do. They package up the debt that companies want to take on, and sell it as bonds. In fact, bonds represent a 35 trillion dollar annual market in the U.S. So we're not talking chicken feed here."

"That's a lot of borrowing!"

"I prefer to think of it as lots of interest being paid. And why shouldn't you and I get some of it?"

"Yeah—bring on the free money," said Larry, remembering their conversation from a few weeks ago.

"But as with everything, you have to understand the risk. The government of some tin dictatorship might default on their loans. Or a company can go bankrupt. It's not as simple as it sounds."

"I get it. Joe's dictatorship might promise a huge interest rate but never pay up at all. While a big, stable company like Coca-Cola may pay me back reliably but not much interest."

"You're getting the hang of it," said Roger.

"I understand investing by lending, how about investing by buying?" asked Larry.

"Again, simple in concept but tricky in practice: buy things which will be worth more in the future or will generate a stream of income while maintaining their value."

"Like Pez dispensers? I heard collectors will pay a fortune for a classic in good condition."

"No, not Pez dispensers, though some people invest in collectibles," said Roger. "Most investors buy stocks, precious metals, businesses, or real estate—to name a few."

"Aren't stocks risky?"

"It depends on how you look at it. If you look at the stock of one particular company on a day-to-day basis, then you may see lots of ups and downs. But the stock market as a whole, taken over long periods of time, like decades, tends to rise."

"You mean I might have to wait decades for my investments to make money?" asked Larry.

"Possibly. But that shouldn't be a problem if you're truly investing for the long run. In fact, a savvy investor would like that. He would get to buy things cheaply while the market is down and then sell at a profit when the market is up a decade later."

"Hey, that's the 'buy low, sell high' thing, right?"

"Correct—though if you start educating yourself on investing, you'll soon discover that most investors do the exact opposite. They tend to buy and sell emotionally rather than invest for the long haul in a disciplined manner."

"They don't stick to the plan, huh?"

"That, or they don't have a plan to begin with."

"So that's all there is to investing, lending or buying? I can't believe it's that simple," said Larry.

"Well, there's certainly more to it once you dig into the details. And the financial services industry has this nasty habit of hiding information and making things complicated. But ultimately, it all comes down to lending, buying, occasionally selling what you bought, and understanding risk. There might be lots of details, but it isn't complicated."

"I've got to run," said Larry, glancing at his watch. "But next time I want to hear some of those details."

Roger smiled. His brother wasn't going to believe this.

Bonds

The financial duo were going upscale today at Public Domain on the corner of Broadway and Alder, a few blocks north of the theater district. For years known as the Portland Coffee House, the shop had remade itself in a high-end image a year ago. The new decor was decidedly spartan, perhaps to avoid drawing attention away from the center island where baristas performed their magic on carefully selected coffees from around the world. Highlighted this week were Burundi Bwayi from Rwanda, Yirgacheffe from Ethiopia, and AA Kiandu from Kenya. Depending on who you listened to, Public Domain had either turned into a hot spot for pretentious coffee snobs or it had inched closer to its original goal of widening Portlanders' coffee horizons with exotic, fair trade product. None of this was a concern to Roger, who had picked the spot strictly because they were known for delivering a thick cup of coffee, the kind whose aftertaste left your tongue happy for hours.

Surprisingly, Larry had spent some time since their last meeting thinking about investing. How cool would it be to tell his buddies he had lent Coca-Cola money? Or better yet, if he had lent to Starbucks, he could use the interest to pay for his daily latte. That would be like getting lattes for free! Of course, he had to have made such a loan to begin with.

"Roger, how would I lend Starbucks money?"

"Thinking of investing in the caffeination of America?"

"There's always a line there, business must be good."

"Good thinking. You buy a bond from a broker."

"Last time you said a bond is a loan, but now it's something I buy?" asked Larry.

"Both. Starbucks doesn't want to deal with thousands of lenders like you at a few hundred dollars a pop. Instead, they work with a financial middleman who lends them the big sum they need and resells the debt as bonds to investors like you."

"So who am I lending the money to, the broker or Starbucks?"

"Starbucks—you just never deal with them directly."

"I still don't see how I buy the bond," said Larry.

"First you need a brokerage account at a place like Charles Schwab, TD Ameritrade, or similar. But do your homework before you blindly pick one," cautioned Roger. "Most brokers are tied into databases which you can browse to find bonds meeting your criteria. You find what you want and then buy it."

"That sounds easy enough—not much different from online banking."

"Yes, the mechanics of it are simple, but making smart choices isn't."

Larry daydreamed playing the role of investor. He imagined owning a portfolio of bonds issued by Coca-Cola, Starbucks, BMW, and others. Instead of paying Visa and MasterCard every month, he'd be receiving interest payments from his favorite companies. No wonder rich guys had a smug look on their faces. The money was coming in instead of going out! Roger's last comment finally registered.

"What's so hard about picking bonds?" Larry asked.

"There are many things to consider—interest rates, default risk, time to maturity, not to mention your goals as an investor."

"My goals? I just want to make some money!"

"Don't we all. However, the first question is whether you can predict the future or not."

"What's that got to do with bonds?"

"If you can predict the future, then you can make lots of money trading bonds. If not, then you're best off buying and holding bonds until maturity."

"How is that?"

"Every bond has a face value, or par value, a time to maturity, and an interest rate."

"Simple enough."

"So let's say you have a $1,000 bond which pays 10% interest and comes due in two years. What have you got two years from now?"

Roger had ordered his coffee black today and took a sip of the heady brew. He wasn't sure he could identify the 'spice cake aromas with white pepper and plantain flavors' as advertised. But it was claimed that coffee surpassed wine in chemical complexity and this definitely was a higher-level taste experience than your run-of-the-mill cup of drip.

Larry was happy Roger finally gave him an example with easy numbers. "At the end of the two years, I get my initial $1,000 back plus I received two $100 interest payments—one each year."

"Right. Now imagine that after the first year the economic climate has changed and a new $1,000 one-year bond is paying 9% interest. Both your old bond and the new bond have the same time to maturity—one year. But are they worth the same?"

"They both have the same face value of $1,000," began Larry, "but I suppose the old bond is a better deal because it will pay $100 of interest in the next year whereas the new bond will only pay $90 of interest."

"Very good, you're really catching on. Another way to look at it is that your old bond represents $1,100 of future money while the new bond only represents $1,090 of future money."

"Makes sense."

"Now comes the tricky part. If the $1,090 of future money is selling for $1,000 today, then shouldn't the $1,100 of future money sell for more than $1,000?" asked Roger.

At first, this notion of selling money was confusing. After all, money was, well, money. You didn't sell it or buy it, you just had it––or not, if you were a guy like Larry. But once he got his head around it, Larry could see bonds from two different perspectives. The first view was that of making a loan with interest. You lent some dollars to Starbucks or whoever now, and they paid you back more later. The second view was that of buying future money—pay X dollars now but take delivery of X plus interest later. They were really the same thing.

"Who knew the phrase 'selling future money' would actually make sense? But I think I get it," said Larry.

"Good—but you haven't answered the question yet. Should the $1,100 of future money cost more than $1,090 of future money costs?"

"Definitely," replied Larry. "You're getting more in the long run so you should pay more now."

"And that's the way it actually works. In our hypothetical scenario you could sell your old bond for more than the new one, in other words more than the $1,000 you paid for it, and realize a profit."

This sounded pretty good to Larry. Buy a bond, earn interest on it for a while, then sell it for more than you paid for it. Ka-ching! Now this was the way to make money.

"I like this plan," stated Larry. "But can it really be that easy?"

"Well, there is a catch. You have to accurately predict where interest rates will be one or more years in the future. Unfortunately, that's hard to do and most people get it wrong, thus losing money instead of making it."

"You know how to burst a guy's bubble," said Larry, knowing that his chance of predicting the future of interest rates was pretty slim.

"So if trading bonds is risky because it's hard to predict the future, then what should I do?" asked Larry.

"The alternative is to buy bonds and hold them until maturity."

"That sounds boring."

"Perhaps, but there's still plenty to get right. You need to understand default and interest risk and plan accordingly."

"By default risk you mean Starbucks might not pay me back?" asked Larry.

"Exactly. Your corner Starbucks may do a good business, but the company as a whole may be heading down the tubes. Maybe they expanded too quickly and are losing money at their other stores. Or there's been a drought in Colombia and the price of coffee beans is about to go through the roof. Or the U.S. Surgeon General is about to release a report that shows caffeine causes cancer."

"How am I supposed to know any of that about Starbucks, much less about any other company whose bond I want to buy?" fretted Larry. "I'd have to read the news all day long."

"That's where the financial services industry comes in. They employ analysts who are supposed to know everything about specific companies and industries."

"But I don't know any of these analysts. Where am I supposed to get my tips?" asked Larry, thinking this was a 'who knows whom' kind of problem.

"Not to worry. Companies like Moody's, Standard & Poor's, Fitch, and others publish their analysts' findings in the form of creditworthiness ratings."

"You mean they actually say if a company or its bonds are a dud?"

"Pretty much. There's some argument as to how impartial the rating firms are. But overall, they do a decent job."

"That makes it easy then. I'll just buy bonds with the highest ratings."

"OK, but then you'll also get the lowest interest because of the inverse relationship between risk and return," said Roger.

"Aaargh! You're always throwing in a twist to complicate things."

"Sorry about that. Savvy investors often have a collection of bonds at different risk and interest levels. Exactly what the mix is depends on their personal tolerance to risk and their plan."

"I get it. A young guy like me might buy riskier but higher-paying bonds because he's got lots of time until retirement in case things go wrong. But someone with just a couple of years to go would want to play it completely safe."

"I couldn't have said it better myself."

The buy and hold plan had sounded boring at first, but Larry could see how it could be interesting. He imagined holding some bonds issued by the federal government. What could be safer than that? Uncle Sam could always raise taxes to get the money for interest payments. Then he'd have some medium-risk stuff from his favorite companies—Starbucks for sure, BMW, Coca-Cola, and whoever made Oberto beef jerky. Lastly, he'd have some high-risk, high-interest stuff from, say, some recently humbled industrial giant trying to make a comeback.

"So far we've focused on how interest rates are determined by risk," began Roger, "but they also depend on two other things. Got any ideas?"

"I hear about federal money policy and interest rates in the news, but I don't understand any of it."

"I'm no expert in that department. But a simple explanation is that the federal government influences economic activity by adjusting the rate at which it lends money to banks."

"But how would that affect bonds?" asked Larry.

"Let's say a company could borrow from the bank at 5% interest. Why should it issue a bond and borrow from you at anything higher?"

"So as the government manipulates bank interest rates, bond rates change accordingly?"

"Exactly. Now how about the third thing that affects bond interest rates?"

Larry thought back to their free money discussion from several weeks ago. There Roger had said that you could earn more interest by lending money for longer periods of time. That had to translate to bonds somehow.

"I suppose bonds with long maturities pay higher interest than those with short ones," he said.

"Very good."

Larry jumped to the obvious conclusion. "So to maximize my return, I should buy the longest maturity bonds I can find?"

"No."

"Why not? I'd just be giving away interest otherwise. That doesn't sound like smart investing to me."

"What happens if the overall economic cycle is such that interest rates are low when your bond matures?"

"Who cares? Interest has been paid over the life of the bond and I've got my principal back. It's all good," claimed Larry.

"But in theory you're a lifetime investor, which means you want to put the returned principal back to work. What are your options?"

Larry saw the problem now. "Darn. All I can buy now is a low-interest bond which means I'm stuck with low returns for the next few years."

"What you describe is called reinvestment risk. It can be a real problem for the long-term investor. Money to invest but nowhere good to put it."

"That won't be my problem anytime soon," observed Larry.

"That may be, but you might think of a way around it anyway."

The whole thing had started with Larry proposing to buy only long-maturity bonds. The opposite would be to buy only short-duration bonds. But that made just as little sense, as those typically had the lowest interest rates. Buy only middle duration bonds? That had no obvious benefit either. That left only one approach.

"Buy bonds of varying maturities?" asked Larry hopefully.

"Precisely. That's what industry experts call a 'bond ladder.' With varying maturities, you reinvest during times of both high and low interest, thereby averaging out the extremes."

This stuff wasn't so complicated after all. And the notion of continually reinvesting when a bond matured was pretty cool. It was almost like a financial perpetual motion machine once you had the system set up. Buy a bunch of bonds, collect interest regularly, roll them over into new bonds at maturity, collect some more interest, roll them over again...

Stocks

A design deadline at work had kept Larry from his weekly finance meeting with Roger. There just hadn't been a free minute anywhere. As usual, his boss had overcommitted to the customer and dumped everything on his underlings at the last moment. Larry worked late several nights grinding out detailed load calculations, updating design documents, printing and re-printing 3-foot-by-4-foot architectural drawings. Thankfully, the newest intern had been stuck with the scale model which would keep him busy all weekend.

Larry wrapped things up Friday night, relieved he'd be able to join his buddies for a hike in the Columbia River Gorge on Saturday. But Roger wouldn't take 'no' for an answer and had insisted they meet before Larry headed out. His compromise was to pick a spot near an I-84 exit as it passed through east Portland on the way to the gorge. Larry found Case Study Coffee courtesy of his car's GPS system. Depending on his mood, he alternated between Arnold the Governator or Seductive Hot Chick voices. This morning it was 'Hasta la Vista, Baby' in an attempt to kick-start his system.

Roger sat at a copper-covered table and observed his nephew shuffle through the door, wearily scan the room, and sleepwalk his way over. Was he safe to drive at this hour?

"Coffee, my kingdom for a coffee," mumbled Larry.

"The usual?" asked Roger as he rose to order.

"Double, no foam," was all the slumped figure could muster.

Larry was in no condition to appreciate the fact that the girl pulling his drink had placed at this year's Northwest Regional Barista Competition. Was there any hope that this morning's meeting would be productive? Roger second-guessed his insistence that they not skip a week. To his surprise, Larry perked up when his cup appeared, even before taking that first sip. Roger wondered whether the effects of coffee were as much psychosomatic as chemical. Time to get things started.

"Do you remember the two primary ways to invest?" opened Roger.

"Sure, lending and buying," replied Larry, hoping this would be the extent of Roger's quiz.

"Last week we covered lending. Today we'll get into buying."

"Ummm," offered Larry, figuring an actual reply wasn't necessary.

"Have you ever bought anything as an investment?"

"My BMW cost lots of money. How about that?"

"Hardly," laughed Roger.

"What's so funny?"

"First of all, you don't own the car."

"I don't?"

"No—the bank owns it. It will only be yours after five years of payments."

"At least I get to drive it in the meantime."

"And secondly, cars are depreciating assets. Every mile you drive and every day that goes by reduces the car's value. That's hardly the characteristic of a good investment."

"OK, OK. I get it. Buying an expensive car on credit wasn't the brightest idea."

"Don't get sore. You walked right into that one and I just couldn't resist. Truce?"

"Yeah, we're good," said Larry, realizing Roger wasn't out to snub him. "But then what do people buy as investments?"

"One of the most common investments is stocks."

"The guys at work are always talking about their stocks. But I don't get it. What are they actually buying? What do they get?"

"Good question. Here's a simplified example you might be able to relate to. Imagine four buddies decide to start a soda distributing company."

"Soda? This is sounding good already!"

"After a while the company owns a bunch of trucks and a warehouse, which is filled with..."

"...Dr. Pepper!"

"I knew this would capture your attention better than, say, a diaper factory," joked Roger.

"Diapers, boring. Mountain Dew, good," declared Larry.

"Let's further imagine that each of the four guys kicked in $5,000 at the start and thus each one owns a fourth of the business."

"OK."

"After a few years of hard work and lucky breaks, the value of the trucks, warehouse, and..."

"...soda..." added Larry on cue.

"...is worth much more than the initial $20,000 the business was started with," continued Roger. "Say the business is now worth $100,000 and one of the guys wants to take his share and go do something new. What does he do?"

"That's easy. He sells his share of the business to someone else."

"Tada! With one simple sentence you've explained what the stock market is about. It's nothing more than people selling partial ownership of companies to one another. The only difference is that most participants in the stock market don't work at the companies they are buying and selling."

Larry chewed on this for a bit and started seeing companies in an entirely new light. Take the case of BMW. He could be a consumer and buy one. Or he could lend them money by buying their bond. Or he could buy their stock and own part of the company itself. Every Beemer that drove by he could say 'my company made that!' But if partial ownership in a small-time soda distributorship went for $25,000, then it would be a long, long time before he could own a slice of a giant like BMW, right?

"How much do these stocks go for?" asked Larry.

"You can see for yourself by checking the listings online or in the paper. But most stocks in the U.S. sell for less than $100 per share."

"So I can become a part owner in BMW for less than a hundred dollars?" asked Larry somewhat incredulously.

"Sure. But realize you're not buying one quarter of the company with that. More like one ten-millionth. But it is partial ownership nonetheless."

"So what's the point?" asked Larry.

"What's the point of what?" said Roger.

"How is owning one ten-millionth of a company an investment? It seems almost useless."

"I agree that one ten-millionth is a pretty small slice of the pie. But you're forgetting how huge the pie is to begin with."

"I know BMW is a big company," said Larry.

"But how much is the entire company worth?"

"I don't know," said Larry, stumped. "A couple of million dollars?"

"Not even close. Say each share sells for $100 and accurately represents what that fraction of the company is worth. Based on that you can calculate the value of the entire company," asserted Roger.

Conversation lapsed until Larry realized this was a mental math question and groaned. If Roger was true to form, he would clam up until Larry provided some sort of answer, so he might as well give it a go. With Roger saying that the price per share accurately reflected the value of the fraction of the company it represented, this was easy. The total value of the company was nothing more than the price of one share times the number of shares. That would be $100 times 10,000,000 shares, which was a one followed by nine zeros or...

"One billion dollars!"

"Bingo! You're part owner of a billion-dollar business," said Roger. "I don't know what BMW is really worth, but large industrial conglomerates are often worth many billions of dollars. So it's not a far-fetched example."

"I get that now," said Larry, "but my $100 share still doesn't amount to much."

"Remember a few weeks ago when I said that investments should appreciate in value, generate income, or do both?"

"Um, sort of," said Larry, even though he didn't.

"It doesn't matter whether your $100 investment represents a big or a small fraction of the company. The only thing that matters is whether it grows and generates income better than if you had invested it in, say, General Motors."

"Didn't they almost go bankrupt a few years ago?"

"Could be. But as long as BMW keeps designing good cars, grows the business, and generates profits such that in a few years the share you bought for $100 is worth $200, wouldn't you consider your one measly share a good investment?"

"Definitely."

Roger knew the stock market was fertile ground for investors and financial pundits. You could read a book a day on investing in stocks – stock-picking strategies, timing the market, mitigating risk, diversifying, tax-efficient tactics, etc. – and still fall behind on the volume of material published each year. Unfortunately, most of it was junk. Some guy would get lucky for a few years, think he was an expert, and publish his version of "How I Made Millions in Stocks." But study after study showed that few people outsmarted the market in the long run. He didn't want Larry to fall prey to all the misinformation out there, believe the hype, and lose his money. But how to tell a kid that although investing in stocks might be part of a good long-term investment plan, 99% of what he'd hear on the subject was garbage? After all, how long did it take until Roger could separate fact from fiction? Even his education on the topic was still a work in progress.

"So, ready to skip a couple pizza nights and buy a few shares of BMW?" asked Roger.

That thought had actually occurred to Larry, but what if BMW didn't do so well over the next few years? Sure, their sports sedan dynasty had begun in 1968 with the model 2002 and the company unveiled new hits every few years. But there had been some duds in there too. The 1974 Bavaria model had been a complete disaster. And it wasn't as though Lexus and Mercedes were sitting on their hands.

"How do I know their stock is going to do well?" asked Larry.

"You don't, plain and simple. Similar to the world of bonds, there are analysts who publish forecasts for stocks. But those are just forecasts and are often based more on the afterglow of an expense account lunch than a real ability to see into the future."

"They're just making it up?"

"It's not that evil. But just think. If analysts really had the ability to accurately predict where stocks were headed, they wouldn't be working as analysts, would they?"

"Hey, that's right. If they really knew what was going on, they'd invest themselves and make a fortune!" said Larry.

"Exactly. But that still leaves the question of how to deal with the risk that the stock you pick doesn't do well. Got any ideas?" asked Roger hopefully.

Larry chewed on this for a bit and had one.

"Well, you could buy an opposite kind of stock at the same time. One that you would expect to behave differently from the first stock."

"That's a good idea," granted Roger. "But the profit from the one added to the loss from the other would always be zero."

"Then how does it work?" asked Larry. "Someone is making money at this, aren't they?"

"It's simpler than you realize. The stock market as a whole reflects the health and size of the economy. Population growth, technological innovation, competition for customers and profits, even the basic human instinct to advance our standard of living—all drive the economy forward."

"So if the economy is good, then stocks grow in value?"

"Generally speaking, yes."

This made sense, but Larry could see an obvious flaw in the plan.

"But the economy isn't always good. What then?"

"That's when you need patience. Historically, those forces of human nature have pushed the economy forward. If you look at 25- or 50-year intervals, the economy and the stock market have always advanced. But year to year there can be significant ups and downs."

"You're going a little cosmic on me now. Are you saying that investing in the stock market is basically a bet that we'll all strive for bigger and better things in the long run?" asked Larry.

"Yes. And a bet in the incredible power of democracy and capitalism."

This sounded like old-timer, 'our system is the best'-style talk to Larry. But it was a firm belief for Roger, who had seen more of life and had a better appreciation of world history. One problem with being young was that you had no perspective with which to see that it was sheer luck you had been born in a country which, despite its many flaws, was based on the ideals of freedom and opportunity for all. Well, that was a topic for another time. Back to more practical matters.

"Have you figured out what to do about that BMW stock yet?" asked Roger.

"No. I still don't know if it is going up or down."

"But you do have an expectation of what the entire stock market is going to do in the long run, right?"

"Only if you're an optimist!"

"Believe it or not, there are investment strategies for pessimists too. But let's stay positive. Assuming stocks as a whole will rise, what would that imply for an investor?"

"Well," considered Larry, "it seems like if you owned a bit of every company's stock, then overall your investment would grow with the market."

"This may be hard to believe, but you just summarized what a bunch of economics PhDs theorized back in the 1960s and 1970s. Of course, they did it with a lot of formulas and complicated language."

"You're kidding," said Larry. "It seems so simple."

"And the proof is straightforward too. For every seller in the market, there is a buyer. The one's profit is the other's loss. So the stock market is a zero sum game if you look at just the buy and sell transactions. If you aren't clairvoyant enough to only pick winning stocks, then over time, the law of probabilities says you will have as many winners as losers. And if that's true, then the only way to make money in the market is to own a bit of everything and wait for the tide to rise."

"If it's that simple, then what are all those guys on Wall Street doing?" asked Larry.

"They're not making money on stocks. They're making money off the people who are buying and selling stocks—selling advice, charging management fees, charging transaction fees, etc."

Larry was having a hard time with the notion that buying a variety of stocks and holding on to them was the way to make money in the stock market. What about all that stock-picking advice in magazines, web sites, and books? "Best Stocks to Buy Now!" must be the most overused headline in the business. Surely someone smart could actually pick the winners. But with so many people shouting, how would you know who was truly the smart one and not just trying to sell a book? The only way to tell the visionaries from the charlatans would be to be a visionary yourself. And just like with the industry analysts, the real visionaries were out making money and keeping it to themselves. After all, who would be dumb enough to give away the goose which laid the golden egg?

"So you're saying that most of what we hear about making money in the stock market is just hype?" asked Larry.

"Sad but true."

"And all I need to do is buy a wide variety of stocks and sit on them for a decade or two?"

"That's the idea. Savvy investors call that a 'diversified portfolio.' The diversification provided by the many different stocks eliminates the all-or-nothing risk you would have with a single stock."

"How many different stocks do I need to minimize the risk?"

"There are many different thoughts on that. Some experts write that it can be done with as few as 15 as long as the choices are made carefully. But it's much easier and safer to just own, say, a piece of the 500 biggest companies."

"That's crazy! At $100 a pop, I'd need $50,000 in order to be diversified. That's never going to happen," groused Larry.

"I've got one answer for you," replied Roger. "Mutual funds."

Mutual Funds

Wet season was here and sandals had been replaced by hiking boots. Many people had the wrong impression of Pacific Northwest winters. In fact, Portland received about the same annual rainfall as most cities on the east coast. The difference was that here it misted from October to May. Locals hardly knew what a thunderstorm was and carrying an umbrella immediately pegged you as a visitor. Temperatures were mild as well. With winter daytime temperatures typically in the mid-forties, all you needed for comfort was a sweater and GoreTex shell. Dealing with endless cloudy days was another issue altogether, though.

Roger's favorite spot on a cloudy day was Floyd's Coffee Shop on Couch Street in the Old Town district. Ample lighting, sandblasted brick walls, refinished wood floors, and uncluttered seating area made the refurbished industrial building a welcome spot to relax. Larry eyed the place with a more critical eye. For one, what was a disco ball doing hanging above the obsolete telephone booth? And what was the purpose of faux wooden columns in every corner? Were they hiding finger-width cracks where the walls were separating?

Nephew and uncle ordered coffee and dug into their breakfast burritos while waiting for the drinks to be prepared. Between bites, Larry tried to get his mind around owning the 500 different stocks required for diversification. Intuitively, it made sense not to risk everything on a single stock, the investing equivalent of putting all your eggs in one basket. Unless you really were clairvoyant, you only had a 50% chance of picking a winner. Actually less, because not all stocks fell in the winner or loser category. Many stocks were just average. Since each stock fell into one of three categories – loser, winner, or average – then the chances of picking a winner were actually down to one in three. But 500 different stocks? How was a person supposed to manage that, much less come up with the money in the first place? Roger had said the answer lay with mutual funds...

"So tell me about mutual funds," prompted Larry. "Because I won't be buying shares in 500 companies anytime soon."

"Very few individuals do," agreed Roger. "A mutual fund is a special kind of company. Instead of making something or providing a service, it exists strictly to make investments."

"OK, but how does that help me invest in 500 different companies?"

"It's a matter of scale. Let's say 5,000 people each put $100 into a mutual fund. How much money would the fund have in play?"

"That's easy," responded Larry, moving a few zeros, "half a million dollars."

"And now let's say the fund splits that half million across 500 different stocks. How much can they put into each stock?"

"Still easy," said Larry, appreciating an easy problem for a change. "One thousand dollars."

"Very good. So by pooling their resources, investors in the mutual fund have ultimately invested in the stocks of 500 different companies even though each of them alone had only $100."

"That's all there is to it?"

"Sort of. The basic idea is as simple as it sounds. But there are thousands of mutual funds out there, each of whom claims to be unique in some way. Understanding their differences and figuring out which might be right for you isn't simple at all."

"Sort of like all cars have an engine and four wheels, but still no two are alike, huh?"

"Exactly."

Larry poured a zesty amount of hot sauce on the last bite of his burrito and chased it with a swig of his latte.

"So how do I pick the right mutual fund?" asked Larry.

"It all comes back to your plan, and perhaps, to your investment beliefs."

"My investment beliefs? Don't go metaphysical on me again."

"Not to worry. But it looks like it's time to explain mutual funds from a different angle."

"OK."

"There's really two groups of people involved in a mutual fund. One are the managers who run the show and make all the investment decisions. The other are investors like you, who are just along for the ride. You provide the money, but the managers determine what gets done with it."

"So I've got to find a fund with managers I can trust?"

"Certainly, though fund managers are typically honest and well-meaning. Plus, the mutual fund industry is regulated by the SEC, the Securities and Exchange Commission, so there is some level of oversight."

"Then where's the problem?" asked Larry, failing to see the issue.

"The problem is that each fund manager has their own set of investment philosophies which they apply to the fund's investments. For example, one fund manager may think he can predict the future and invests only in stocks he thinks will be hot in the upcoming year."

"And if he was wrong, I've lost my investment."

"Yes. In fact, the variety of fund philosophies is overwhelming. You've got actively managed funds which pick stocks they think will do well. You've got passive funds which buy and hold. There are sector funds which invest in specific business sectors, like energy or transportation. Then there are funds to invest in bonds, or just government bonds, or just corporate bonds, or only small businesses, or only big businesses, or only international businesses, or only Asian bonds, or only Australian gold companies, or any combination you can think of."

At first Larry didn't see this as much of a problem. After all, choice was good, right? But then it dawned on him that choice was only good if you knew what you wanted. And if you could really tell the choices apart.

"I get what you're saying," said Larry. "Choices just confuse things for those who don't understand their needs."

"Spoken like a true investor," marveled Roger.

"So how do I know what a fund's strategy is?"

"That's where it gets a bit murky. Every fund publishes a prospectus which by law requires it to lay out its investment strategy. But there's a lot of wiggle room in what they say."

"How's that?"

"For starters, they say as little as possible and use only the most general terms."

"Sure, so no one can pin them down!"

"Then there are the SEC rules which only require a certain percentage of the fund's assets to be used as promised in the prospectus. Some percentage can be invested at the discretion of the managers. Usually that is done wisely so as to better manage cash flow, but things happen."

Larry was starting to see the benefits of mutual funds. Perhaps the biggest benefit was that they provided diversification for people like himself with limited money to invest. And in theory the fund manager did all the research to figure out what to invest in. That way he wouldn't have to analyze hundreds of companies himself, something that sounded about as much fun as a trip to the dentist. But the more he thought about it, the more it looked like he had only replaced one problem with another. Instead of analyzing all the companies and bonds out there, he now had to analyze thousands of mutual funds instead. And if their prospectuses were as obtuse as Roger said, then it might be even more difficult to know what's what. This investing business sure required one to do their homework. Damn!

"Do I really have to read every mutual fund's prospectus to figure out which to invest in?" asked Larry. "There's got to be a simpler way."

"Definitely. Only the wonkiest investors enjoy settling in with a good prospectus. Most common folk, me included, consider reading a prospectus a sure-fire way to fall asleep."

"So what do I do?"

"As always, first have a plan. Know whether you want a bond fund, stock fund, active or passive management, etc. Narrow it down as much as possible."

"And then?"

"Then start browsing reports from market research firms like Morningstar, Lipper Weiss Ratings, Standard & Poor's, or others. Those are examples of companies which analyze mutual funds, categorize them, and present their performance statistics in a standard format so they are easy to compare."

"Are these reports online?" asked Larry, an idea popping into his head.

"Often."

"Then I can just look them up, sort them by performance, and pick a few off the top. This will be easy!"

"You should read a few prospectuses first," cautioned Roger.

"Why bother? Search. Sort. Invest. And let the money start rolling in. Piece of cake."

"It doesn't work that way," said Roger. "Every prospectus contains the following caution for good reason: 'past performance is no guarantee of future results.' "

"So you're saying the performance ratings are fake?"

"No, the performance ratings are real. But while they are 100% accurate about the past, they are 0% predictive about the future."

"Completely accurate yet totally useless. How can that be?"

"All right, here's an example to illustrate the problem. The annual returns of all the mutual funds can be averaged together, right?"

"Sure."

"And how many of them will have beat the average?"

Was this a trick question? A few outliers on the winning or losing side could shift the average far from the midpoint. But if most values were evenly clustered around the average, then half would be below and half above.

"Can we assume even distribution?" asked Larry.

"Getting technical, huh? Sure, assume an even distribution."

"OK, then half the funds beat the average."

"Correct. Now of those which beat the average, how do you know which were smart versus just lucky?"

"Um, those that were above the average a couple of years in a row?" asked Larry hopefully.

"Maybe—but still not a guarantee. A fund might do well several years in a row because its strategy is well matched to the current economic situation. But as soon as the economy shifts, it won't do so well at all. You might be tempted to pick a fund that is about to head downhill."

"So the bottom line is that there are no guarantees," summarized a dejected Larry.

"And don't ever let anybody tell you different," counseled Roger.

Roger felt he had communicated the essence of mutual funds well enough for Larry to start doing some research on his own. And there was plenty of information out there for people who wanted to educate themselves. Between hardcopy materials at the public library and electronic reports online, an investor could make a career out of reading reports and fine-tuning their plan. But they had skipped over one important aspect of mutual funds.

"You know," began Roger, "instead of investing in a mutual fund, you could start one of your own."

"What do you mean?" asked Larry.

"You remember the two groups of people involved in a mutual fund, right?"

"Sure, the investors and the managers."

"All I'm saying is you could start a fund of your own and be on the manager side of things."

"In theory, but I don't think anyone will trust me with their money," observed Larry.

"Probably true. But just for the sake of argument, imagine you did start a mutual fund."

"OK," said Larry, visualizing himself in a power suit and corner office, barking buy and sell orders to his subservient minions.

"Naturally you're making lots of money for your investors," kidded Roger. "But what do you get out of it?"

Larry was momentarily stumped. Sure, the investors' money was growing, but what was the payoff for the manager? The manager could have some money invested too. But why would someone with enough savvy to invest successfully and run a fund bother with the hassle? Why not just grow their money on their own without dealing with all those pesky investors?

"I suppose the manager could charge for his services?" ventured Larry.

"Bingo! Just as mutual funds vary widely in terms of investment success, they also vary in the fees they charge."

"What kind of fees are we talking about?"

"Ah, that's where the manager's creativity sometimes really shows! Some funds have 'sales loads'—fees which are assessed every time you put money in or take it out. Then there are management fees, 12b-1 fees, and the catch-all 'other expenses.'"

That corner office was starting to look better and better. Advertise to bring in thousands of investors, skim a few bucks off each one, and pretty soon it would be good-bye Burger King, hello five-star restaurants. But Larry knew that was just a dream and that he'd be on the investor side of the equation for a long time to come.

"It sounds like all those fees could make a dent in the growth of my investment," observed Larry.

"Definitely. Let's ignore sales loads as there are plenty of no-load funds out there to choose from instead. What do you think the other fees add up to?"

"I don't know, one percent?"

"That's actually a pretty good guess. The lowest in the industry are down around one tenth of one percent, and the highest are probably several percent."

"That doesn't sound too bad."

"Don't be so casual about fees," warned Roger. "You pay them in good times and bad. Over time, especially for the long-term investor you're supposed to be, it can really add up. Thousands of dollars, in fact."

"I don't know," ventured Larry. "Even if I had $10,000 invested in a fund, a 1% fee is only $100. That's not much."

"Maybe not the first year. But what would the cumulative fees have been over, say, 20 years?"

Larry did the math. "Two thousand dollars."

"Now we're talking real money. Not only did you lose that to fees, but the $2,000 didn't get to compound on itself either. You're losing twice, in a sense."

"Yeah, $2,000 would buy a fair amount of goodies. I guess it does add up."

Time to wrap things up, thought Roger, and give his nephew something to work on. He had some errands to run and Larry had to get to work.

"Think you've got a handle on mutual funds now?"

"Oh yeah, no problem," said Larry, reaching for his jacket.

"Then here's a little homework assignment for you."

"No one said anything about homework."

"Find a low-cost mutual fund which invests in the 500 biggest companies in America and tell me about it at our next meeting."

"No problem," said Larry, figuring he'd easily get that from one of his older coworkers.

"But no cheating," admonished Roger, "do the work yourself."

Grr!

Financial Advisors

"Did you do your homework?" asked Roger.

"More than that, even. I went to a finance seminar!"

"How did that happen?"

"Oh, I get invited to them all the time," said Larry casually. "I think I got myself on a mailing list somewhere."

"And?"

"Why didn't you tell me about index funds? This guy said they are much better than regular mutual funds."

"I suppose he had a few favorites for you to invest in too?" asked Roger.

"His company does. They have an index fund which invests in big companies like you wanted me to find for my homework assignment."

"It's good to hear you're expanding your financial horizons," began Roger, "but what do you really know about these funds? Do you understand how they work, what the risks are, their associated expenses, that kind of thing?"

"Um, no," conceded Larry. "But all the graphs sure made it look like people were making money with them."

"You're a classic investor," said Roger. "All exuberance and no diligence. It's got to be the other way around if you want to succeed at this game."

The two sipped in silence, neither wanting to continue the conversation where it was headed. Larry didn't like being told he was impulsive and didn't think things through. Roger was wise enough to know that saying exactly what was on his mind would only push Larry away, rather than increase his confidence and curiosity. Sometimes you just had to zip it and take a different approach.

Roger let his eyes roam around the shop while he deliberated where to take things next. Cafe Velo was a small place with few tables as it catered mostly to the downtown take-out business crowd. As the name implied, the business was originally a bicycle-based operation. The owner operated a pedal-powered cart at strategic locations around town. Weekdays saw the cart at high-traffic downtown corners. Saturdays he pedaled it to the farmers' market. Sundays you could usually find him at the art fair under the Burnside

Bridge. This shop at Sixth and Pine was a new joint venture with baker Lauretta Jean. Though Jean owed her initial notoriety to pies, her quiche was starting to build a loyal following. Portlanders were foodies too.

Roger had an idea for a new approach.

"Do you do your own taxes?" he asked.

"Yup, and I hate every minute of it," answered Larry. "Add this. Subtract the larger of the two of that. But only if you had a hangnail during the last quarter of the year. Those forms are pure torture."

"We're in agreement on that one. I used to do my own, then used a tax guy as my situation became more complicated."

"It would be nice to dump it all in someone else's lap, that's for sure."

"You have to be careful who you pick though, and understand the hierarchy of tax professionals."

"What hierarchy?"

"At the bottom there's you."

"I'm no tax professional," pointed out Larry.

"True. But it hasn't stopped you from doing your taxes, right?"

"Right."

"Then you've got tax services like H&R Block, or others, which are designed to handle the average tax return, but nothing too fancy."

"Yeah, they seem to pop up all over around January."

"After that come your CPAs—Certified Public Accountants. They can handle more complicated stuff, although many just use a better version of tax software than you would normally find at the local office supply store."

"I always rib the accountant at work by asking where his pocket protector is."

"Good one! And then at the top of the heap you have accounting firms where, at least in theory, the collective expertise of their many tax professionals is applied to your return."

"That's not how it works?"

"Not necessarily. It depends on how much they value your business and whether they think you're on the ball yourself. Often junior associates do the bulk of the work under the supervision of a senior partner."

"Architecture is the same way. Junior guys like me crank the numbers while the chief architect does the presentations and gets the credit."

"Such is life."

They paused to watch a bunch of suits yapping about 'supply chains, order fulfillment, and inventory turnover' get complicated drinks and drift out again.

"It's the same in the financial world," continued Roger.

"What is?"

"That there's a hierarchy of professionals with different aims and skills."

"OK."

"Only it's a lot more dangerous for the customer."

"How do you figure?"

"How do the tax professionals make their money?"

Larry gave it a shot. "I guess they charge for their time or by the job."

"Generally, yes. The finance world has 'fee only' professionals too. But others not only have fees, they demand a percentage of your total assets each year."

"Sneaky. As my money grows, so does their cut—even though they didn't do any extra work."

"In good times and in bad, just like a marriage."

There sure were lots of different financial types running around, thought Larry. The older guys at work were often on the phone with their broker. His parents met with some kind of financial advisor twice a year. Then you had all these guys hawking finance seminars on paid programming TV. There was an E*TRADE office a few blocks over. And the few times he read a business magazine, he noted ads from various 'wealth management' companies.

"Financial services must be a big industry," observed Larry.

"I read recently that it's over $1 trillion per year."

"That's big bucks. So who are all these guys?"

Where to begin. "Well, you've got your banks."

"Yeah. Home of my emergency fund and maybe a few CDs," said Larry, proving he had been listening.

"Good! Then you've got brokerage houses."

"Like Schwab or TD Ameritrade?"

"Right. Brokers handle the buying and selling of financial instruments like stocks, bonds, and mutual funds. Discount brokers try to provide that service for minimal cost. Others offer investment advice and additional services."

"They hold my stuff for me too, right?"

"That's right—no more stock certificates in your safe deposit box. The broker holds your investments in what's called 'street name.' Nothing is printed and nothing physical changes hands. Databases are merely updated to reflect who owns what."

"Let's hope they do backups every night."

"They sure do. In fact, many computer innovations were driven by the needs of the financial services industry."

"So we've got banks and brokers. What else?" asked Larry.

"Then comes the universe of financial advisors, large and small. You've got independent professionals, franchises, professional partnerships, and even mega-firms with thousands of employees."

"Franchises, like Burger King?"

"Why not?" replied Roger. "For example, Edward Jones is a franchise. Mr. Jones developed an effective way to provide financial services to suburban communities and packaged that as a business plan anyone can buy."

"That sort of takes the mystique out of it," lamented Larry.

"Don't let that color your judgment. If you're a typical investor, the local franchise guy may give you more personalized service than the uppity firm which doesn't acknowledge your existence until you have a million dollars to invest."

Larry remembered when his company had sent him to a trade show and put him up at a swank hotel. It was obvious he couldn't afford the place on his own and the desk clerk had been decidedly cool.

"I hate attitude. A million bucks just to get in, huh?"

"That's the exception—don't get me wrong. The important thing is, with so many financial service opportunities out there, you should pick what matches your needs, not what you stumble across first."

"And understand how they're going to make money off me."

"You're really coming along," complimented Roger.

Larry was going to run across many financial advisors of one sort or another over his lifetime. Roger knew it would be difficult to tell the good from the bad. Although credentials didn't insure integrity or aptitude, at least you knew the person had met a basic set of requirements.

"What kind of degree did you graduate with?"

"I've got a Bachelor of Science."

"So you've got a degree in BS?" joked Roger, thinking of the more common interpretation of those two letters.

"I thought about going on, but wanted to earn some money first."

"You know what an MS is, don't you?"

"A master's degree?"

"It's just, um, More Stuff," said Roger, unwilling to use the cruder word, "and the PhD is the same Piled Higher and Deeper."

"Yeah, some of those eggheads at college were full of 'stuff,' as you call it."

"The financial world has its own alphabet soup of designations."

"Like CPAs?"

"And you should be familiar with the more common ones so you know who you're dealing with."

"Makes sense."

"Those are the Chartered Financial Analyst (CFA), the Chartered Financial Consultant (ChFC), the Certified Financial Planner (CFP), and the Certified Investment Management Analyst (CIMA)."

"These aren't diplomas you buy out of the back of a comic book, are they?"

"No, these credentials take real study and often require a number of years of experience before you can be certified."

"Schools grant these degrees?" asked Larry, never having run across them.

"Most are self-study courses administered by professional organizations. But don't underestimate their difficulty. Some have full-day exams and you'd be surprised at the breadth of material which is covered."

"So I could become a CFA if I wanted to?"

"Sure, but you better want it pretty bad as it requires passing three 6-hour exams and four years of experience in the finance industry. And their historical pass rate for all three exams is only a hair over 50%."

"Half who try don't make the cut?"

"At least not on the first try. Now the CFA may be the toughest of the lot to earn, but you get the idea. On top of that, to keep the certification, many require ongoing education every couple of years. So it's no picnic."

"Who knew?" said Larry.

"Of course, you can't just have faith in anything you see printed on a business card."

"What do you mean?"

"Well, some terms are generic and don't confer any special training—like investment advisor."

"Or financial consultant?"

"Exactly. Before you work with someone, you should check out their credentials to understand their area of expertise and to verify they are up to date. After all, anyone can order business cards overnight on the internet."

"You see a scam artist under every rock!" chided Larry.

"What you earned over years can be lost in a day if you work with the wrong people," warned Roger. "Caveat emptor."

"Caveat emptor?"

"That's Latin for 'let the buyer beware!' "

All this talk of financial advisors made Larry wonder whether he should be looking for one. But at this early stage he hardly had anything to invest, much less additional with which to pay for advice. Then again, wasn't Roger sort of acting as his advisor for now? Not only that, Roger didn't need to be paid. In fact, he was covering the tab for coffee at all their meetings. Maybe Larry was more astute about getting something for nothing than he realized!

"So when does one need a financial advisor?" asked Larry.

"It depends. You need one now if you have no inclination to learn on your own or are lacking the discipline to get started."

"That's the old me. I'm reformed now."

"You're starting to come around, I'll grant you that."

"But you didn't like how I did my homework, did you?"

True, but Roger wanted to keep things positive. Pointing out Larry's deficiencies was hardly the way to keep him motivated.

"I'm glad you discovered index funds," began Roger. "Can you tell me a little about them?"

"Um, not really," admitted Larry.

"An index is a number which tracks some kind of financial activity. For example, the Standard & Poor's (S&P) 500 index tracks the average value of the 500 largest companies in America."

"So it's like a snapshot of the health of the economy?"

"Exactly. And there are indices for just about anything you might be interested in. For example, the Dow Jones Industrial

Average (DJIA) tracks 30 commonly traded American stocks, the Hang Seng Index (HSI) tracks Asian stocks, etc."

"Is there an index for snack food stocks?"

"Not that I know of, but they do get quite specialized. For example, the XAU index tracks the performance of gold, silver, and copper mining companies."

"Too bad," said Larry, wishing for a junk food index to invest in.

"An index fund, then," proceeded Roger, "merely invests in the same things and in the same proportions as the index which it tracks."

"That's it?" asked Larry. "They just buy the same stuff that the index tracks? No investment research? No timing the market? No predicting where interest rates are headed?"

"None of that. As stocks, bonds, or whatever go in and out of the index because they do or don't meet the index criteria, the fund buys or sells accordingly."

"You don't need much brainpower to do that," commented Larry.

"That's why index funds have some of the lowest expenses in the industry," agreed Roger. "With the right index, you get tremendous diversification at low cost."

Index funds were fine and good, thought Larry, but then what were all those financial types doing? After all, almost every financial services ad hyped how smart they were about picking the right investments. It seemed to come down to whether you believed it was possible to pick winners or not. If so, then find an advisor and trust their judgment. If not, then pick a few index funds which provided diversification and hope the economy ran strong.

"So do I only need an advisor if I want someone to pick my investments for me?" asked Larry.

"Hardly. A good financial advisor will educate you, help you fine-tune your plan, analyze your financial situation, lay out plausible scenarios for the future, and more."

"Sort of like a financial guidance counselor?"

"Precisely—with the caveat that the advisor wants to increase their income as much as they want to increase yours."

"I get it, I get it," said Larry. "Buyer beware."

Real Estate

The day was unusually balmy for fall so Roger took an outdoor table at the Cloud Seven Cafe. The outdoor seating area overlooked Jamison Park, a popular oasis in the industrial area turned new urban called the Pearl District. The park featured a variety of outdoor art and natural rock features which had initially attracted skateboarders. The city curbed their activities by running water across the rocks at random times. Serendipitously, the runoff collected in a natural depression which kids and dogs loved to play in. Now water was a permanent feature, causing locals to refer to the park as their community pond.

It was too cold for wading but there were plenty of twenty-somethings with strollers out for fresh air. Roger tried to remember what he had been up to in his mid-twenties. That would have been around 1975, several years into his job as a postal carrier. Nothing much came to mind so most likely he had been living day to day, getting his job done, and enjoying the first year of his marriage. For sure he hadn't been thinking about investing, although marriage had triggered an interest in the future. Was the current generation all that much different?

"Are your friends starting to plan for the future any?" asked Roger.

"It's a mixed bag. Some have their act together and others don't."

"Does anyone ever talk about how to save and invest?"

"Not so much that. But there's plenty of talk about buying houses. It seems everyone wants to get a place of their own and quit paying rent."

"Ah, the great American Dream."

"As soon as someone is in a serious relationship or gets married, they start looking for a house. They all say it's a great investment."

"It can be, but there are also many myths about home ownership."

"One of my married buddies says that since they're not making any more land, it's got to appreciate in value."

"He must not have been to Detroit lately where they're turning deserted city blocks back into farmland."

"But the population is expanding, don't we need more houses?"

"In theory, but real estate is complicated. It's regional. It's affected by government policies. It's sensitive to demographic trends and generational preferences. Lastly, it's cyclical, meaning it goes through periodic highs and lows."

"That doesn't seem to be stopping anyone," observed Larry.

"Just proof that people believe in the myths rather than the reality," replied Roger.

"And the reality is?"

"When you buy a house you are committing to large monthly payments on a non-diversified asset whose value depends on an environment you don't control."

"Well, if you put it that way..."

"Not only that, young buyers are at a mobile period in their lives, most apt to move, and thus have the biggest risk of being hurt by a down cycle in real estate."

"Did you forget your happy pills this morning?" teased Larry. "You're all gloom and doom."

"Just trying to set the record straight. For every real estate success story, there's a corresponding sob story. Most of the success stories are luck. And many of the sob stories could have been avoided if people were more realistic."

"So is there a perfect time to buy a house?" asked Larry.

"Not exactly. But in general it's good to wait until you're at a stable point in your life, especially career-wise, and are willing to commit to a neighborhood that will serve your needs for many years."

The Pearl District was a perfect example of how far the real estate pendulum could swing in just a few years' time. Created by the forces of urban renewal, the 1990s saw the area change almost overnight from warehouses and light industry to condos, loft conversions, and retail. Between a robust economy and demand exceeding supply, property values rose and many committed to hefty mortgages in the latest trendy part of town. But now, just a decade or so later, the picture was a lot less rosy. Overbuilding in other areas of Portland had resulted in a real estate glut. Combined with a stagnant economy, real estate prices were severely depressed and many now owed more on their mortgages than their properties were worth. Precious few had seen it coming or sidestepped the financial punch.

Larry saw his uncle as unreasonably down on home ownership. The guy was a regular contrarian, dismissing what most thought was a good idea. Like this housing business, for example. At least with a mortgage you were building up equity. Everyone knew that. And his friends said you got to deduct mortgage interest from your taxes. That sure seemed better than the alternative.

"So you're saying I'm better off paying rent forever rather than buying a house?" baited Larry.

"Not forever. But getting into real estate isn't a slam-dunk decision like some make it out to be."

"My house-buying friends use rent-versus-buy calculators on the internet to prove that buying a house is a better deal," Larry said.

"Those calculators grind numbers in a vacuum. If you ignore risks and other factors, then there's almost always some point in the future where the numbers will show that buying has a financial advantage over renting."

"So where's the problem?"

"Aside from the fact that most people overestimate how soon they will move again and don't hit the payoff point?"

"Yes."

"OK, here's one. If you buy a house too early, as in you used all your savings for the down payment and signed up for the maximum mortgage your income allows, then you have concentrated your risk and can't afford any drop in income."

"But what if I kept my emergency fund intact and used other savings for the down payment?"

"If you also purchased less house than your income allows, then you might be in good shape."

"Only might?"

"There's always the question of what else you could have done with your money."

"What do you mean? I'm either paying the rent or paying the mortgage."

"You're forgetting the down payment. It may grow faster invested elsewhere."

"Yeah, but with mortgage payments I'm building up equity every month," said Larry, thinking he had found a hole in Roger's logic.

"That's true. But in the first few years of the typical mortgage, only about 25% of your payment actually goes to equity. The rest is interest."

"But that's tax deductible!" claimed an exasperated Larry.

"Lots of people think that means it doesn't cost them anything. But that's false. The interest deduction is dependent on your tax bracket. Those with smaller incomes see less benefit. And then only if they itemize deductions."

"So if I do the standard tax return, I don't get a mortgage interest tax deduction? That doesn't seem fair."

"You still get the standard deduction then. But regardless, unless you're in a stratospheric tax bracket, you're on the hook for the bulk of the interest payment. You personally are feeding the bank, not the government."

"You sure know how to paint a lousy picture," accused Larry.

"I just want you to see that it's not as simple as most people make it out to be. Whether to rent or buy is a complex financial and emotional decision."

Larry wasn't convinced that real estate was a bad investment. His dad used to subscribe to *Forbes* magazine and each year's Top 400 list of richest Americans included several real estate tycoons. Somebody was making money in real estate. How were they doing it?

"What about all those 'Get Rich with Real Estate' books?" asked Larry.

"They're good for inspiration, I guess, and provide a platform for people to brag about how well they've done. But the fundamentals of making money in real estate aren't hard to understand."

"What? Weren't you just telling me how people buy too much house at the wrong time?"

"I was. But you're confusing home ownership with real estate as an investment activity. Those are two different things."

Larry was intrigued. He had no desire to own a home at this stage in his life. He had better ways to spend his time than mowing the lawn, cleaning gutters, or regrouting bathroom tile. But the term 'real estate as an investment activity' had a cool ring to it. That's what those Fortune 400 tycoons must be doing.

"You say it's easy?" asked Larry hopefully.

"The principles involved are easy to understand. What's difficult is insuring all the right conditions."

"And those principles are..."

"There are fundamentally only two real estate money-making strategies—appreciation and rents."

"Appreciation is where you sell it for more than you paid. And rents is where you get money for its use. Right?"

"Exactly," said Roger. "Let's start with appreciation. You can get that several ways. One way is to buy early in an area with growing demand. When demand exceeds supply, prices go up and you make money. Easy, right?"

"If you know where there's going to be demand soon." Though by now Larry knew this could just as easily work against you if you didn't predict the future accurately.

"Another way to get appreciation is by adding value. That's what developers do. They take raw land and build something on it. As long as there is someone willing to buy at a price higher than the cost of development, they make a profit."

"Sort of like flipping a property where you buy it cheap, fix it up, and sell it for more," said Larry, thinking of a cable show he watched now and then.

"See, the concepts involved aren't complicated. The hard part is knowing when, what, and where to buy, and how to improve the property such that a profitable sale is guaranteed. Miss on any one of those and you'll have an expensive lesson in bad judgment."

That did sound like a lot of things to get right all at once. And unlike other investments you could buy into for small amounts, real estate required lots of money up front. Maybe plan B was easier.

"What about rents?"

"Again, the fundamentals are simple. You get regular payments for the use of a property you own, or at least control."

"Control?"

"Let's say you bought a property with a small down payment and financed the rest with a mortgage. You won't own the property until the mortgage is completely paid off. But in the meantime, you control how the property gets used."

"But how do I make money if I'm paying a mortgage?"

"That's the trick. You'll make money only if the rents you collect exceed the cost of mortgage payments, taxes, and maintenance."

"That doesn't sound easy," acknowledged Larry. "A couple of frozen water pipes and you lose money that month."

"You bet. Financing costs, unexpected maintenance expenses, tenant vacancies, and property tax hikes are always nibbling away at your positive cash flow in a rental. That's not to say it can't be done. It's just not as simple and risk-free as many books make it out to be."

Roger hoped he had done a good job framing the difference between home ownership and real estate investing. Home ownership sometimes turned out to be a good investment. But first and foremost, it was a commitment to a community and a lifestyle. Real estate investing, on the other hand, should be approached like any other financial opportunity. It only made sense once you were educated on the subject, understood the risks, and determined that it fit into your overall financial plan. Everything they had talked about so far assumed direct ownership of property. But there was another option.

"Do you remember the fundamental premise of a mutual fund?" asked Roger.

"Sure. Multiple investors achieve diversification by pooling their money. And depending on the type of fund, they may benefit from professional management."

"Wow! That sounded like it came straight out of a finance book. You're really getting the hang of this."

"Oh yeah," beamed Larry.

"As it turns out, there is a similar investment mechanism for properties called the Real Estate Investment Trust, or REIT, for short. REITs pool investor money to purchase properties and hire professional property managers to run them."

"So my $100 investment can buy a fraction of a shopping mall, for example?" asked Larry.

"Not only that; by law, REITs must distribute at least 95% of their annual income to shareholders. As a result, they tend to generate higher dividends than other investments. Just keep in mind this comes to you as taxable income, not capital appreciation, though REIT shares can rise in value too."

This was starting to sound good. No big investment required, professional managers did all the work, and Larry got the income.

"Where's the catch?" asked Larry, having acquired some of Roger's financial cynicism.

"First off, there are two kinds of REITs—equity REITs and mortgage REITs. As you might expect, mortgage REITs invest in mortgages. In other words, they lend money to home buyers."

"That doesn't sound much different from a bond mutual fund," commented Larry.

"Indeed, they are quite similar, though each has peculiarities investors should be aware of."

"And equity REITs?" prompted Larry.

"Those invest in real properties and then hopefully manage them for a profit."

"What kinds of properties?"

"Some deal with only one kind of property, like malls, for example. Some specialize in urban properties. Some are tied to a geographic region. Some only invest in hospitals. Others have a bit of everything."

"So a REIT could pick bad properties just as easily as a private investor."

"Sure. As a REIT investor then, you need a plan. Are you betting that drive-in theaters are the income producer of the future, or do you want to limit your risk by diversifying across many kinds of properties?" asked Roger.

"It always comes back to the plan, doesn't it?"

"Who do you want in charge?" asked Roger. "Yourself, or the indiscriminate hand of fate?"

Roger felt the conversation had drifted away from the financial basics that a guy like Larry needed at this stage in life. If you considered home ownership a lifestyle choice rather than an investment, then few could be considered real estate investors. Most investors didn't branch out into real estate until later in life when they had a few extra assets to deploy. Time to bring the conversation back to something Larry could use relatively soon.

"Do you know the most often stated financial lie in America?" asked Roger.

Larry pondered a moment. "The check's in the mail?"

"Good try. But I was thinking of how people say they own a home."

"Don't they?"

"Not really," explained Roger. "What most people have is a mortgage, often the biggest debt of their life. And until it is paid off, the bank owns the home."

"So all the houses we see are owned by banks?"

"Not all the houses, but certainly a lot of them. Think about it, how many so-called 'homeowners' do you know without a mortgage?"

"No one, really, except for maybe older folks," agreed Larry. "But I thought the bank only owned the house if it went into foreclosure."

"Nope. The bank, or some other financial institution, has legal title to it as long as there is a mortgage outstanding. Foreclosure just means that the current mortgage holder has quit making payments and the title holder is enforcing their legal right to the property."

The notion that you could make mortgage payments for years and still not own your home was unsettling. Weren't you steadily increasing your percentage of ownership with each payment?

"Aren't people building up equity as they make mortgage payments?" asked Larry.

"They might be, but equity and legal title are two different things," replied Roger.

"Only might? So I can make payments and not build up equity? That doesn't make sense."

"Officially, your equity in a property is the difference between what it is worth and what you still owe. If the property rises in value, your equity will increase whether you're making payments or not. Though I wouldn't recommend skipping any."

"And going the other way," observed Larry, "if the property drops in value, you might lose equity even while you're still making payments."

"Correct. A property is called 'underwater' when it is worth less than the amount still owed on the mortgage."

"Wait, isn't a property worth at least what you paid for it?"

"That's a frequent wish. But the sad truth is that anything is only worth what someone will pay for it now. What you paid and what you owe have no bearing on its current value."

Larry frowned as the ramifications of Roger's last statement sank in. Buyers didn't care what you paid or if you still owed on what you were selling. They strictly looked at what similar items were going for and took the best deal. If you were dumb enough to overpay when you bought, or the world had changed such that equivalent things were now cheaper, then you were going to take a loss. This was true for houses, cars, stocks, bonds, and even Pez dispensers.

"So to make money on a house," said a chastened Larry, "I both have to buy it cheaply and sell it at the right time."

"Makes you wish for a crystal ball, doesn't it?"

Mortgages

Larry had paid close attention to what his friends said about real estate since the last meeting with Roger. Maybe some of his uncle's financial hardheadedness was rubbing off, because much of what they said seemed based on weak logic. Regardless, all of them thought their mortgage was a foolproof wealth-building tool—assuming you didn't skip any payments. They clearly weren't on the same page as Roger on that one. What was up with that?

"Last week you made it sound like having a mortgage is risky business," began Larry.

"It can be," replied Roger. "A mortgage is the biggest financial transaction most people will ever engage in, yet they are woefully uninformed on how they really work."

"Such as?" fished Larry.

"The first thing to realize is that a mortgage is a form of leverage."

This was a new one. "Leverage?"

"Sure. Financial leverage is a technique by which you amplify gains or losses."

"I don't get it."

"Then let's do a simple example. Say you put $10,000 down on a $100,000 house and finance the rest with a $90,000 mortgage."

The numbers were easy so Larry had no problem following along.

"Imagine the house appreciates 10%. What is it worth now?" asked Roger.

"That's easy. The house is now worth $110,000."

"Very good. Let's say you sell at $110,000 and pay off the $90,000 mortgage. What have you got left?"

This was still easy math. "After the sale I've got $20,000 left. I doubled my money!"

"Exactly. Your property appreciated only 10%, but your $10,000 down payment appreciated 100%. That's leverage," said Roger.

Larry took a sip of his double tall and noted that his uncle always ordered drip coffee and took it undoctored. Was this a reflection of his frugality or did his taste buds lean to bitter rather than sweet? Today's meet was at The Fresh Pot, just a few blocks from Larry's office. Quick service and free WiFi made this a midday break favorite, not to mention the ever-changing artwork. The owners supported local artists with free wall space. Larry wasn't the type to visit a gallery, but he did check out the works of the week when he visited. Past collections had ranged from M.C. Escher-style political protest drawings to Picasso-style cubist oils. This week featured landscape photos turned surrealistic by digital color mutation.

This leverage business was sounding pretty good. Let the house appreciate a bit and then double your investment. Do that a few times and the initial $10,000 would be serious dough in no time. But there was an obvious catch.

"What if the house doesn't appreciate?"

"That's where leverage will bite you," replied Roger. "Let's do the example the other way around. Assume your $100,000 house lost 10% of its value and you had to sell. What happens?"

Larry worked the problem out loud. "Well, losing 10% of its value means I sell it at $90,000. After paying off the mortgage I have no money left at all. Everything is gone, including my $10,000 down payment. Ouch!"

"So you see that leverage can work to your detriment as well. In the second case your house depreciated 10% but your investment depreciated 100%. In other words, you lost everything you put in. If that's not risky, I don't know what is."

Larry understood the leverage example but something just didn't make sense.

"If mortgages are so risky," he asked, "then why are so many in such a rush to buy a house?"

"That's a good question," said Roger. "Many people just don't understand the details. You can't make intelligent decisions about something you don't understand. Then there's the national obsession with home ownership. There is this misguided notion that you're not a success unless you live in a home. Lastly, many are misinformed on the tax benefits of home mortgages."

"Yeah, all my house-buying friends talk about how their interest payments are tax deductible."

"I wouldn't be too sure," cautioned Roger.

"Are you saying mortgage interest isn't deductible?"

"It can be. But as it turns out, the majority of Americans hate doing taxes so much that they don't bother with itemizing their deductions. They just take the 'standard deduction' which you get whether you have mortgage interest or not."

"My friends must be itemizing because they're saving big bucks."

"Are they?"

"Well, at least they say they are," Larry said unconvincingly.

"I'll be the first to admit that if you qualify for itemizing deductions and actually do it, you'll get a tax break," clarified Roger. "But you'd be surprised at how small a tax break it really is."

"Don't you get to deduct the entire interest from your taxes?"

"Ah, that's the popular misconception. Here's how it actually works. But maybe we should use some real numbers to make it realistic?"

Larry struggled to parse the photo visible behind Roger's head. The incomprehensible slowly gave way to a maple tree in fall silhouetted against a sunset, albeit with all colors replaced by their spectrum complement. Probably a one-click option in PhotoShop.

"I'm ready," said Larry, straightening in his chair.

"We need an annual income for the example, so let's say you're making $60,000 a year."

"All right, a promotion!"

"Without a mortgage, your taxable income is your gross income minus the standard deduction, which recently was around $6,000 for single persons. So your taxable income is what?"

"Easy. $60,000 income minus the $6,000 standard deduction comes out to $54,000 of taxable income."

"If I remember the tax tables correctly, your tax would be right around $9,700."

What type of mind would retain such arcane facts? Larry decided not to comment. "Uh huh," was all he said.

"Now let's say you had a $150,000 mortgage at 6% interest. What amount of interest would you pay in the first year?" asked Roger.

Larry knew how to simplify this one. Six percent of $100,000 was $6,000. The mortgage in question was one and a half times $100,000, therefore the interest would be one and a half times $6,000 as well.

"Nine thousand dollars."

"Good. Now let's add in $1,000 of property tax, which is also a deductible expense, making a total of $10,000 in deductions. What's your taxable income this time around?"

Larry did the math out loud. "$60,000 income minus $10,000 in deductions comes out to $50,000 of taxable income."

"Correct. And the tax on that is right around $8,700, or $1,000 less than when you didn't have a mortgage."

Saving $1,000 on taxes looked like a really good deal at first. But after a while, Larry saw it in a different light.

"So I had to commit to a mortgage and shell out $10,000 in interest and property tax to save $1,000 on my income tax, is that it?"

"Pretty much. Your mortgage payments for the year were actually more than $9,000 because you both paid interest and built up some equity. And you theoretically had other homeowner costs like maintenance and insurance."

This wasn't turning out to be so clear-cut after all. There were too many interrelated factors which made it hard to say with any certainty whether buying a home was a smart move. Let's say you did buy a home. Your taxes might be lower, sure. But your down payment was locked into the property and due to leverage, might grow handsomely or disappear altogether. And in the meantime you had to mow, paint, and maintain.

Renting was equally two-sided. While your down payment was available to invest elsewhere and you had zero maintenance responsibilities, you weren't building any equity and could be paying more in taxes. But you could move anytime you wanted and there was no leverage risk.

"I think people buy homes because they want to and use the tax argument to justify it," concluded Larry.

"Could be. Humans are great at justifying an emotional decision with questionable logic."

There was a lot more that Larry needed to understand about mortgages if he was going to be a savvy home buyer in the future. But how to interest a guy in a problem he might not face for a couple of years? Roger had an idea.

"You mentioned that some of your friends are purchasing homes," probed Roger, "and that they're claiming to be the financial experts."

"That's right."

"Maybe it's time you set them straight."

"What do you mean?"

"Your friends may only have a rudimentary knowledge of the mortgage industry and could benefit from your advice."

"My advice? What do I know about mortgages?"

"Pay attention and it could be a lot."

Additional mortgage facts didn't sound too interesting to Larry, but the thought of sticking it to some of his know-it-all friends was attractive.

"OK, I'm game. But what's to know? Isn't a mortgage just a big loan for a long time?"

"Not necessarily," replied Roger. "The traditional mortgage is the 30-year, fixed-rate loan. But there are many variations."

"Such as?"

"There's the Adjustable Rate Mortgage, otherwise known as ARM. That's where your interest rate changes based on some financial index."

"You mean the payment can change from one month to the next?"

"Yes, and very rarely does it work in your favor."

"That sounds risky," observed Larry. "Why would someone take one of those?"

"Humans are optimists?" asked Roger rhetorically. "Mostly an ARM is a way to buy more house than you can presently afford combined with a bet that interest rates won't rise or that your income will."

"It still seems risky, not knowing in advance what the full financial obligation is going to be."

"Well said! Another variant is the interest-only mortgage with balloon payment."

"Balloon payment?"

"Here's how it works. The mortgage is only for, say, five years and during that time all you pay is interest. Payments are smaller than a conventional mortgage since there is no principal component in the payments. But after the five years are up, you owe the full amount borrowed. That's the balloon."

"That doesn't make sense. Where are you supposed to get the money to pay the balloon? If you had that kind of money, you wouldn't have needed the mortgage in the first place."

"The balloon is usually covered by taking out a traditional mortgage at the end of the five years."

"It sounds like the only people making out on these deals are the banks," observed Larry.

"That's pretty much the gist of it. With real estate deals often in the hundreds of thousands of dollars, it should be no surprise that financial institutions are highly creative in structuring loan products that make them lots of money. While it's true that some of the more esoteric loans help people get into a property they couldn't afford otherwise, it's typically the case that the risk goes to the borrower and the profits to the lender."

"That's your 'no free lunch' theory?"

"Yes. And I'm sticking to it."

Larry tried to remember what kinds of mortgages his friends had. "I think my friends have traditional fixed-rate, 30-year mortgages. So they're safe, right?"

"Your friends made safer choices than some of the other loan offerings, but the devil is in the details."

"Like what?" asked Larry, knowing he was going to get the details whether he wanted them or not.

"For example, at a 5% interest rate, you pay almost the same amount in interest as you do principal over the life of the loan."

It took a moment for the significance of this to sink in. "You mean my friends pay back double what they borrowed? That's not a mortgage, that's a loan sharking deal!"

"Not only that, in the early years they're paying mostly interest. It isn't until the 22nd year that more than half of each payment goes toward equity."

Larry was stunned. "Twenty-two years until they're paying more to themselves than to the bank? Is that legal?"

"Completely legal," assured Roger, "and even tame compared to some of the other mortgages we talked about earlier."

Some of the larger prints around the room drew Larry's attention away from the conversation, but it wasn't their artistic merit that was doing it. Rather, he wondered whether the mega-printer they used for architectural drawings back at the office could produce prints at this level of quality. If so, he was looking at a money-making opportunity. How hard could it be to snap a few photos, mangle them digitally, and hang them on the wall here with a $300 price tag. Easy money!

"So what might you recommend to your friends to reduce their mortgage costs?" asked Roger, bringing Larry back to the conversation.

An easy one came to mind right away. "Obviously they should shop around for the lowest interest rate."

"And what else?"

This took a bit more thinking. Earlier they had talked about how every loan had four components—the amount lent, the interest rate, the time over which it was to be repaid, and the payment amount.

"I suppose they could go for a shorter time period?" said Larry.

"Very good. If your friends took out a 15-year mortgage, also at 5%, then although their monthly payments would go up by about half, the overall amount they pay back would only be one and a half times what they borrowed."

"So with the 15-year mortgage, my friends would take more pain each month but save significantly overall."

"Anything else?" asked Roger.

Larry tried to think of other strategies his friends could use to reduce their mortgage costs.

"We've already monkeyed with the interest rate and the loan duration. About the only other thing they have control over is the amount of the loan to begin with."

"Good observation. As we saw in the 5%, 30-year loan, every $1,000 they avoid borrowing saves them another $1,000 in interest paid. But there is one more strategy they can apply."

Larry concentrated, but nothing came. "I'm stumped."

"Here it is. Your friends can take the 30-year mortgage with its smaller payments, but pay extra in months where they have spare cash."

"There are no such months!" joked Larry.

"They should check the terms of their mortgage, but typically extra payments are applied directly to principal."

"So where's the benefit? The monthly payment is still the same."

"Extra payments reduce the remaining loan balance. This means next month's payment has a higher percentage of principal than it would have otherwise."

"I see. It's another play on the four components of a loan. Since the interest rate and payment are unchanged, then reducing principal ahead of schedule also shortens the life of the loan."

"Exactly. In the $200,000 at 5% example, adding $25 extra per month chops about one and a half years off the 30-year mortgage."

"Big deal," complained Larry. "No one holds a mortgage for 30 years nowadays."

"You're missing the point," said Roger. "Focus on the interest."

Larry mulled that one over but no clear insight would crystallize. "Total interest for the life of the mortgage is reduced?"

"Correct. But here's a better way to look at it. Any prepaid principal is money your friends will never have to pay interest on ever again—whether they hold the mortgage to term or not."

Larry couldn't help but chuckle. "It's like cheating the bank, only legal. Here the bank was counting on all that interest and now they won't get it. Score one for the little guy."

"Score one for the little guy who applies extra cash to the mortgage regularly," qualified Roger. "Too bad there aren't that many of them."

Taxes

Leaves crunched underfoot as Larry worked his way across the Portland State University campus in the southwest corner of the city. He didn't come this way often and made a few wrong turns before finding the Meetro Cafe on the ground floor of the King Albert building. Roger knew the campus well from attending PSU Vikings women's basketball games at the Stott Center a few steps away. The trash talking superstars of the NBA and the elbow throwing men's college game didn't capture his interest anymore. But the women's game was still one of finesse and teamwork and a joy to watch. At only $7 admission, it was cheap entertainment.

Tonight's game started at 7:00 pm, plenty of time to meet Larry after work and still get a good seat before the tip-off. Roger figured it was time his nephew learned a bit about the great bogeyman of finance, taxes. Most Americans considered the U.S. tax code a complicated and unavoidable evil. And at 70,000-plus pages and growing, they were correct in that assessment. But you didn't have to be an accountant or tax law junkie to understand the principles at work.

"You know of the two certainties in life, don't you?" asked Roger.

Larry had heard this one before. "Sure, death and taxes."

"And you're aware that the federal income tax is progressive?"

"That means larger incomes are taxed more than smaller ones."

"Sort of."

"They aren't?"

"Depends on how you look at it. In one sense, high-income earners are subject to the same tax rate as low-income earners."

"No way. Everyone knows rich people pay higher taxes. Unless they have a really good accountant, that is," added Larry.

Roger ignored the jibe about the rich not paying their fair share of taxes. While true that they could afford the best tax professionals, the actual numbers indicated it wasn't helping any. The top five percent of earners in the country paid well over fifty percent of income taxes collected by the government.

"Our tax system is based on ranges, or brackets, of income. For example, we currently have brackets from zero to $7,500, then

$7,500 to $30,000, and so on all the way up to incomes of millions of dollars a year."

"That would be nice!"

"The guy earning millions of dollars per year pays the same amount of tax on his first $7,500 earned as the guy who earns only $7,500 a year total."

"So when does the rich guy pay more tax?"

"Each income bracket has a progressively higher tax rate, which is why we call it a progressive tax system. For example, the tax rate on dollars zero through $7,500 might be 10% while the tax rate on the next range of income might be 15%."

"So the rich guy pays the same tax as the poor guy for the first bit of income and only pays a higher tax on the additional income."

"You've got it. The tax rate on the last dollar you earn, namely the dollars earned in the highest tax bracket, is called your marginal tax rate."

Larry vaguely recalled a dinner discussion with his dad once about marginal versus average tax rates but the details were long gone.

"But that's not the average tax rate, right?" Larry asked.

"Correct. Here's an easy example to see the difference. Imagine your first $50,000 of income is taxed at 5% and the next $50,000 of income is taxed at 10%."

"OK."

"What tax would you pay on a $100,000 income?" asked Roger.

This wasn't too hard. 5% tax on the first $50,000 was $2,500. 10% tax on the second $50,000 was $5,000. Then add the two together.

"Total tax due is $7,500," answered Larry.

"So if you paid taxes of $7,500 on a total income of $100,000 then what was the average tax rate?"

"7.5 percent."

"Very good. So in that example, the marginal tax rate was 10% while the average tax rate ended up being 7.5%."

"How high does the tax rate go?"

"At present, earners in the highest income bracket get taxed at 35%."

"At present?"

"Tax rates are set by our elected officials in congress. They rise and fall to reflect the country's needs and political climate. Over the last century, the highest marginal tax rate has ranged from a low of 15% all the way up to 94%."

"You mean there was a time when people only got to keep six cents out of every dollar they earned? That's outrageous!"

"We're talking marginal tax rate here. Not every dollar was taxed that aggressively, only the last dollar earned."

"Still, that's a big hit."

"Agreed. Be careful who you vote into office!"

As far as Larry was concerned, taxes were something to be ignored until about one week before April 15th. The last few years he had gotten a refund which was pretty nice. Of course, a bigger refund would be even better. Maybe Roger had a few ideas.

"Got any tips on how to increase my tax refund?" asked Larry.

"Tax refunds are a loser's game," replied Roger.

That made no sense. When it came to a tax refund, 'super-size me' sounded just fine.

"How can it be a loser's game when the government is paying me?"

"The government isn't paying you anything. It is returning back to you taxes overpaid throughout the course of the year."

"So? Bigger is still better."

"Look at this like an investor. When you overpay taxes in advance, what you've really done is made a zero-interest loan to the IRS. What investor in their right mind lends their money at zero percent interest?"

"No one, I guess," said Larry.

"That's why refunds are a loser's game. If you didn't overpay taxes with each paycheck deduction, then you could invest the extra money yourself and make some profit."

Or spend it, thought Larry. "But I never see that extra money, so what's the point?"

"As it turns out, you control how much tax is deducted from each paycheck. Paycheck deductions are determined by the W4 form you give to your employer."

"The W4 form? I haven't run across one of those."

"You probably filled one out when you started work and haven't adjusted it since. But it's something you should review each year."

"I hate tax forms. The instructions don't make sense and you never know if you've got it right."

"All true. But in this case the IRS makes it easy by providing a withholding calculator on the web. It lets you fine-tune your paycheck deductions so that you get more money in your pocket sooner."

"But no more refund, huh?"

"The money can be working throughout the year for you or for the IRS. Which do you want?"

Roger looked around the room. Unlike its slick commercial counterparts elsewhere in Portland, the Meetro Cafe was distinctly a student hangout. Gray-painted walls, mismatched furniture, and aging equipment behind the coffee bar attested to the low-budget nature of the business. But what it lacked in professionalism, it made up in youthful energy and innocence. Groups of students clustered around tables talking animatedly, seemingly immune to the perils of drinking coffee this late in the day. Besides, they wouldn't be hitting the hay for many hours yet. After all, on college time this was just getting to be midday.

"So you're not a big fan of tax forms?" said Roger.

"That's for sure! It's just one big alphabet soup of gibberish to me."

"Yeah. Most people aren't comfortable with exclusions, adjustments, deductions, exemptions, and credits."

"See what I mean? Why can't they just use plain English?"

"That's what you get with a tax code enacted by a bunch of senators who are mostly lawyers to begin with. But it's really not that complicated."

"Tell that to a few hundred million Americans on the night before taxes are due," complained Larry.

"True enough. The details can get complicated. But the overall picture is straightforward and once you understand it, it helps bring some of the details into focus as well."

"I don't know. I have trouble even with the 1040-EZ form."

"There's some IRS humor for you, naming the 'easy' tax form the 1040-EZ. Oxymoron is more like it. But I'll bet I can get you to understand the whole process without a single diagram."

"You're on," said Larry, doubtfully.

"OK. First you start with all your income—absolutely all the money you received during the year."

"Even the $100 my mom gave me on my birthday?"

"That too. It won't be a problem because personal gifts are not taxable to the recipient—that's you."

"Lucky me!"

"The next step is to subtract from that total all the things the government, in its great wisdom, has decided not to tax."

"There are such things?"

"Sure. And the list is quite long. In addition to gifts, you get to subtract things like insurance proceeds, home sale profits, municipal bond interest, retirement fund contributions, moving expenses, student loan interest, and more."

"Let me get this straight. All those things are subtracted from my income and don't get taxed at all?"

"Correct. The details are spelled out in various tax forms that you should understand before subtracting things willy-nilly. But the framework is simple."

"Who knew Uncle Sam was so generous?"

"He'll be taking his bite soon enough, just wait."

"No doubt," said Larry.

Roger briefly considered the irony of today's subject in this setting. Though many students worked part-time and were required to file a tax return, between meager salaries and various educational deductions, their taxes often didn't amount to much. It wouldn't be until they entered the full-time working world that taxes might start making a noticeable blip on their financial radar. And if they achieved half the success their education was intended to provide, the bite might become painful.

"Now we'll get technical for just a second. What we just subtracted from your income are the exclusions and adjustments. What we're left with is called your adjusted gross income, otherwise known as your AGI."

"I can handle that."

"Believe it or not, we get to reduce your AGI even further before we figure out how much tax you owe."

"That works for me, but why didn't we do that in the first step?" asked Larry, seeing this as yet another example of unnecessary complexity.

"Good question. The stuff we subtracted in step one was removed in its entirety. For example, all of the $100 your mom gave you was subtracted from your income. How much we subtract in the next step depends on all sorts of special case rules."

115

"Sounds complicated."

"I won't lie to you," said Roger. "This is where the devil is in the details. But even so, the principle is simple. In the first step we subtracted 100% of things allowed by the government. In the second step, the percentage to be subtracted is determined by special formulas."

"I get it. We're getting less of a deal than in step one, but still reducing the amount we're going to be taxed on."

"Step two subtractions are called exemptions and deductions."

"This is where my friends subtract their mortgage interest, right?"

"Yes, and maybe other things as well. Other deductions might include state and local taxes, charitable contributions, or medical expenses."

"You mean a root canal is tax-free?"

"It depends. Medical expenses can only be deducted if they exceed some percentage of your AGI."

"So it's only if I'm really sick that I get the medical tax break?"

"Essentially, yes. That's a good example of the special rules for deductions. Each one has different qualifying criteria."

"I know, read the fine print."

"Or have your accountant do it," offered Roger. "Continuing then, after subtracting all the things you're allowed in step two, we're left with what is called your taxable income."

"Now comes the bad news, I'll bet," said Larry, foretelling where this was headed.

"Yes, it's finally tax time, so to say. But the good news is that we're calculating tax on a number much reduced from what we started with, right?"

"I sure hope so."

"We look up your taxable income in the tax tables to determine your tax liability, but we're not done yet."

"We're not?"

"Nope. Now we get to subtract credits."

Larry was confused. "You mean after we figure out our tax, we get to reduce that tax some more?"

"Hard to believe, but true. Credits represent activities the government wants to encourage."

"Such as?"

"There are credits for first-time homeowners, hybrid cars, home energy upgrades, and education expenses, to name a few. But keep in mind that they change with the political tide. Credits come and go at the whim of whoever is currently running the show in Washington."

"Now we're done?"

"We are done. After subtracting all the applicable credits from your tax liability we end up with tax due, which is what you actually end up paying."

Larry performed a quick review in his head. It wasn't all that complicated after all. Start with all your income. Subtract exclusions and adjustments to get the adjusted gross income. Next, subtract qualifying deductions and exemptions to get the taxable income. Look up the taxes on that. Finally, subtract any applicable credits to get the tax due. What he had previously imagined as a complicated flow chart with multiple paths branching and reconverging had been reduced to a linear process.

"It's not as simple as a flat tax, but it sort of makes sense once you boil it down to just four steps," said Larry.

"Wait till you have some money making money for you. Then it gets more interesting again," countered Roger.

Tax-Smart Investing

Mention the dreaded word 'taxes' and most people thought about money that was going to be taken away from them or perhaps never get to see in the first place. Contrarian as always, Roger had a different take on the subject. It wasn't that he found the nation's tax laws particularly interesting. Rather, once understood they represented opportunity for financial gain. And just like compounding, the effects could be sizeable after a period of several years. How to get Larry to see the opportunities?

"I think it's time you learned about unearned income."

Unearned income had a nice ring to it. "How do I get some?"

"You've got some right now," dangled Roger.

Initially all Larry could think of was his salary, which given how hard he worked, was most certainly earned income. His savings account earned interest, but that wasn't earned in the working sense.

"Savings account interest?"

"Good! Most free money opportunities are considered unearned income since you aren't being paid for your labor."

"Hey, I had to work hard to put that money aside."

"That's true. You worked for the money initially. But once invested, the money works for you and its benefits are considered unearned."

"Do stocks and bonds generate unearned income too?" asked Larry.

"Those are the classics, I suppose, and have two forms of income associated with them. Bonds pay interest while some stocks pay dividends. And both can generate capital appreciation if sold for more than they cost you."

"So money I make selling things for a profit is unearned income as well?"

"Yes. But the government makes the distinction between short-term and long-term gains and taxes you accordingly."

"Short and long?" asked Larry.

"Short-term gains are profits from things you have owned less than a year. Long-term gains are from things you have owned more than a year."

"I don't see why the government would care how long I owned something as long as they get their tax money in the end."

"It's more of a philosophical distinction," admitted Roger. "One interpretation is that if you're buying and selling within a year's time, then you are speculating. Alternatively, if you are holding on to something for longer than a year, then you are making an investment which benefits the economy, stimulates growth, enables world peace, and so on."

"World peace? That's a stretch."

"Hyperbole, perhaps. Regardless, the general sentiment in congress is that long-term investments are good and should be encouraged. Thus long-term capital gains are taxed at a lower rate than short-term gains or earned income."

"So I pay less tax on my savings account interest than my salary?" asked Larry.

"Unfortunately, interest is considered a short-term gain so it is taxed the same as earned income. But sell some stock you've had for more than a year and now you're a member of the low-tax club."

"How low are we talking?"

"Long-term capital gains have been taxed at 15% the last few years."

This long-term capital gains ploy was starting to sound good. Hold stuff for more than a year and pay less taxes than the guy working for a salary. No wonder the rich got richer. They were the ones with enough money to invest for more than a year at a pop and thus got the tax breaks.

"So to keep more of the money I make, I've got to make it in a different way," observed Larry.

"The more you can replace salary income with long-term investment income, the less tax you pay," agreed Roger.

There was a lengthy silence as Larry traced the implications of this statement. If you took this to its logical extreme, then the cheapest way to live would be to have no salary income and subsist totally off of long-term investment income.

"So living off of long-term investment income is actually the most tax-efficient way to go."

"Exactly," said Roger. "And if you plan it right, that's what we call retirement."

"That's a big if."

"Well, let's put some numbers on it to give you some incentive. Say you built up a nest egg of $500,000 over the course of your career and it generated 5% of long-term gains per year. What would be your taxable income?"

"That's easy, $25,000."

"And after taxes?"

"If the long-term capital gains rate is still 15% when I finally get around to retiring," assumed Larry, "then after tax I'm left with $21,250 to spend each year."

"You have now performed more retirement planning than most Americans," said Roger. "Congratulations!"

Today's meet was at the midtown Seattle's Best coffee shop on 6th Avenue. Roger always got a chuckle when people claimed to patronize the chain as an anti-Starbucks statement. Little did they know Seattle's Best was a wholly owned subsidiary of Starbucks. Your money ultimately lined the same pockets regardless of whether your cup sported a green logo or a red one. If anything, the strong opinions proved the effectiveness of branding. Starbucks sold itself as upscale while Seattle's Best tried to appear affordable and accessible. Roger drifted to one of his favorite subjects, namely how much consumer behavior was influenced by marketing and whether that was fundamentally good or bad... After a few seconds he caught himself and got back to business.

"What if I told you there are some investments which aren't taxed at all?" asked Roger.

"No way! You mean there's some truly free money out there?"

"I hadn't thought of it that way, but yes, some money is totally free. You do nothing to earn it and it doesn't get taxed."

"Are you going to let me in on it?" asked Larry hopefully.

"It's called municipal bonds," explained Roger. "Municipalities, like Portland for example, borrow money to build sewers and such. You buy their bonds and earn interest on them."

"That doesn't sound any different from the bonds we talked about a few weeks ago."

"The difference is that the federal government wants to encourage investments in municipalities and doesn't tax the interest."

"What a deal! First I get free money when the bond earns interest and then I get to keep all of it because it isn't taxed. Where do I sign up?"

"Not so fast," admonished Roger. "It's not that simple. First, you want to be sure that the bond has a good rating. In other words, the municipality issuing the bond has to be a good credit risk."

Thinking of a municipality as equivalent to a business entity with an investment rating was a new concept for Larry. But it really wasn't that weird—Portland took in money through taxes and provided various services in return. That was just like a business if you replaced taxes with fees.

"Municipalities are sort of like service businesses, then?"

"That's a good way to think of them. And like other businesses, they can be managed well or poorly. For example, New York City almost went bankrupt in 1975."

"The whole city?" asked Larry incredulously.

"And Orange County in California filed for bankruptcy in 1994. Their bond holders took it in the shorts."

Larry also hadn't heard of that one, even though Orange County was a lot closer to home than the east coast.

"Next you need to consider the after-tax return of the investment," continued Roger.

"What's to consider? There are no taxes so I get to keep it all."

"True. But just because municipal bonds are tax-free doesn't mean they are a better investment than taxable bonds."

Larry knew he was heading into mental math territory but asked the question anyway. "How do you figure?"

"Let's say a taxable bond paid 5% interest. What would you earn in a year on a $1,000 bond?"

"Fifty dollars," answered Larry promptly.

"Good. Now let's say you paid 20% federal tax on average. What would you have left after taxes?"

Larry worked it through. "20% of the $50 interest is $10, which means I would have $40 left after taxes."

"OK. Now let's say you had a $1,000 municipal bond which paid 4% interest. What's your after-tax amount now?"

"Well, 4% of $1,000 is $40 and since the municipal bond isn't taxed, I get to keep all of it."

"So assuming equal investment risk, what can you conclude about municipal versus taxable bonds?" asked Roger.

From the earlier example, it was clear to Larry that for someone who paid 20% tax on average, a 4% tax-free municipal was equivalent to a 5% taxable bond.

"You have to know your tax rate in order to compare taxable and tax-free bonds?"

"Exactly. Because it's not about what you earn, it's about what you keep."

It was fitting that they talk about taxes at this Seattle's Best as it was near several government buildings. The Wendell Wyatt Federal Building and three federal courthouses were only steps away. IRS agents, Veterans Administration employees, lawyers, marshals, court clerks, and government employees of every stripe made this a busy spot. And that was only the federal government. Add in the many City of Portland offices nearby and it was a wonder any private money was spent here at all. This shop was sustained by tax-funded salaries, a perfect example of the trickle-down effect of government spending.

"Does your company have a pension plan?" asked Roger.

"You must be kidding!" replied Larry. "I don't think anyone offers pensions anymore."

"You'd be surprised. Many civil servants, military personnel, teachers, and other unionized employees are still eligible for pensions."

"Yeah. But if what I read in the news is true, even those won't be around much longer."

"Probably true. Pensions are going the way of the dinosaur. Why should an employer guarantee your financial future when he can push that problem onto you instead?"

"You're not working up to another personal responsibility lecture, are you?" asked Larry.

"Nope. I was working up to tax-advantaged retirement savings plans."

"That's a mouthful. Can you say that in plain English?"

"The government encourages saving for retirement through various tax incentives."

"It still sounds complicated."

"Let's look at the incentive part first. Remember that exercise where we calculated that you had to earn $2,500 in salary to afford $2,000 of after-tax expenses at Starbucks each year?"

"I remember. But the numbers have improved since you started buying me coffee once a week!" noted Larry.

"Mooching has its benefits," conceded Roger. "But what I was getting to is that the government encourages saving by not taking any taxes out of earnings you put into qualified retirement savings plans."

"No taxes? I keep it all?"

"None—up to certain limits, at least."

"What are these plans called?"

"The most common plans are Individual Retirement Accounts, typically referred to as IRAs, or 401k plans, so named after the section of the tax code which defines them."

In the taxable world and assuming 20% income taxes on average, every $1,000 earned resulted in only $800 which could actually be spent. Unless you put the money into a tax-advantaged IRA or 401k plan. In that case, $1,000 earned resulted in an equivalent $1,000 of savings. This sounded too good to be true.

"There's got to be a catch, right?" asked Larry.

"Nothing about tax incentives is ever simple," stated Roger, "and you should read the fine print carefully, as always. In this case, the major restriction is that you can't touch the money until you're 59½ years old."

"And if I do?"

"Then you get whacked with a 10% early withdrawal penalty in addition to having to pay income tax on what you take out."

"I see why these are called retirement plans. You have to keep your mitts off the money for a long time if you want to avoid the penalties."

"That's negative thinking," commented Roger.

"You can put a better spin on it?"

"Maybe now is the time to mention that earnings in the account aren't taxed."

The eyebrow blip Roger delivered with this last statement made clear that it was an important detail. But how exactly?

Larry reviewed what they had discussed earlier. Income and short-term capital gains were taxed at the highest rates. Long-term capital gains were better because they were taxed less. It stood to reason that investment earnings which weren't taxed at all were even better yet. All that was pretty obvious. But he and his uncle were past the obvious now. There had to be something else.

"No tax on earnings is good," ventured Larry.

"Think time," hinted Roger, trying to put his nephew on track.

"The free money will grow faster?"

"Exactly. Since IRA and 401k plan earnings aren't taxed, every dollar they generate is available for compounding. Over time it can make a big difference."

Larry hoped to avoid another math problem by giving a noncommittal answer. "Uh huh."

It worked. "Depending on interest rates, tax rates, and how consistently you add money during your career, a tax-advantaged account can end up with 30% to 100% more money than a taxable account."

"More money just because I parked it in the right kind of account?"

"That's the result of compounding over the course of a typical 40-year career minus the insidious effects of taxation."

Larry was unknowingly coming around to his uncle's perspective on taxes. For all the bad, there were pockets of opportunity—provided you knew about them and actually took advantage of them.

"Guess I better check this out once I've got my emergency fund and insurances squared away."

"Now you're talking," encouraged Roger. "Surprisingly, almost 50% of working Americans fail to take advantage of this tax break."

"Go figure."

Start a Business

The good intents of interior designers notwithstanding, it was hard to overcome the built-in limitations of the average coffee shop. Commercial real estate rates kept shops small and seating crowded. Direct entry off the street brought frequent gusts of cold air as customers came and went. The coffee-as-entertainment philosophy required baristas to make drinks in public view. This resulted in a constant clamor of coffee presses, milk steamers, and shouted orders.

Some days you wanted something more refined and this was one of them. The pair met at the Palm Court lounge in the lobby of the Benson Hotel at 309 SW Broadway. Often referred to as Portland's Grand Hotel, the historic Benson was the epitome of elegance and refinement. Dark paneling, elegant furnishings, and impeccable service all contributed to the relaxing experience. Even a simple drip coffee was a special event when served in a thin-walled china cup in this setting.

"What kind of driver are you?" asked Roger.

"Pretty good."

"That's what I expected you to say. What American male doesn't think he's a good driver?"

"Well I am. I haven't had an accident yet."

"That may only mean you're lucky, not skilled. Don't you know some bad drivers who are still accident free?"

"Yes," begrudged Larry.

"Don't get sore. I was just trying to point out that you never really know how things stand unless you measure them."

Larry knew there had to be a money angle in this conversation somewhere, but damned if he could see it. "My driving has something to do with money?"

"Well, it is interesting how young males think they're the best drivers while the insurance industry, which actually tracks accident statistics, assigns them the highest risk. But that's not what I was leading up to."

"And that is?"

"A good measure of a person's financial situation is their net worth."

"I did a worksheet on that once. That's where you take the value of everything you own and subtract everything you owe and see what's left over."

"Exactly. How did it look for you?"

"Um, not too good," confessed Larry.

"Pretty average there, I'd say. Many Americans have a negative net worth which means their debts exceed the value of what they own."

"That's me."

"Sorry to hear that," consoled Roger. "But with time and effort you'll be able to reverse that situation."

"That's the plan," said Larry, thinking of all he had learned so far.

The only background noises in the lounge were the muted conversations at sparsely scattered tables. The clientele here was definitely higher end than at their usual haunts. Customers sported tailored suits and designer watches rather than rack suits and electronic gadgetry. These people had 'people' who dealt with schedules and email. How fitting that they would be talking about net worth.

"Can we agree that net worth is a good measure of financial stability?" asked Roger.

"Yeah, sure."

"Then here's the question. What category of Americans has the largest number of net worth millionaires? In other words, people who really own stuff worth a million dollars or more which isn't offset by a corresponding debt."

Larry sure didn't know any millionaires. Some of his older coworkers had big houses, but it's unlikely they were paid for.

"Sports professionals?"

"Nope. Try again."

"Movie stars?"

"Nor them. Those groups both have high visibility and may make lots of money. But they are small in number compared to the total population of Americans, which is now over 300 million."

"I give up then," said Larry, tired of guessing.

"The millionaire's club is overwhelmingly made up of small business owners," said Roger.

"So if I want to be a millionaire, I should start a business?"

"Statistically speaking, that's got better odds than picking hot stocks or winning in Vegas."

"I don't know," doubted Larry. "I sort of like getting a paycheck without all the extra hassles."

"That has a certain merit. But it misses the key insight which motivates successful business owners."

"They think differently?"

"Sort of. Consider the relationship with your employer."

"What about it? I work and they pay me. Though not enough," he added as an afterthought.

"True. But think of it in terms of a trade."

"Well, I'm trading my time for money."

"Any other benefits?" asked Roger.

"We've got a health plan."

"That's good. But it's the same as money. You could just get paid more and buy health insurance on your own. Any others?"

"Not really."

"OK. Now what is the business owner getting for his time investment?"

"I sure hope he's getting more money!" said Larry.

"Let's assume he is. But isn't he getting some other benefit?"

"If there is, I don't see it. If anything, he's got more headaches than if he just had a regular job somewhere else."

Roger could see his nephew wasn't ready to make the leap from employee to business owner anytime soon. Was he going to have to spell it out in bold print or could he get him to make the mental leap on his own? He approached it from the other end.

"Larry," said Roger, "imagine that some long-lost relative died and left you his business."

"What a headache!"

"Let's make it better then. In addition to being profitable, the long-lost relative had perfected the business to the point where it pretty much ran itself without his day-to-day intervention."

"Well, that's different," claimed Larry. "Now I've inherited a cash machine instead of a headache. That would be pretty nice."

"Indeed. Now can you identify what motivates business owners?"

Finally the insight hit. Business owners weren't just trying to earn a buck today. They were also building a cash machine for tomorrow.

"Now I see why they always talk about 'building the business.' That's just biz-speak for building a cash machine so that you eventually don't have to do the work yourself."

"Exactly," said Roger. "There may be an entrepreneur in you yet."

Simon Benson, namesake of the hotel, had been a serial entrepreneur. His business efforts included a general store, logging, commercial real estate, shipping, and the hospitality industry. Not everything was a success, though. He endured two prosperity to poverty cycles before achieving the success that would last his lifetime. Was that proof that starting a business was risky or that persistence paid off?

"People start businesses for all sorts of reasons," continued Roger. "It's not always about the money."

"Yeah. Some people just can't stand to work for someone else."

"Not surprisingly, those people are also often hard to work for because they lack people skills. You've probably run across a few of those yourself by now."

"I've been pretty lucky with bosses," said Larry. "But some of my friends work for complete imbeciles."

"Sometimes it's a product idea which motivates a person to start a business."

"Like Google?"

"Sure, but it doesn't have to be high tech. It can be as simple as cupcakes, or duck calls for hunters."

"Someone has to make wiffle balls," observed Larry.

"Don't forget pet rocks!" added Roger. "But there are many straightforward business opportunities out there even if you aren't passionate or expert about something yourself."

"Like what?"

"Franchising, my boy, franchising," intoned Roger.

"That's your business secret?"

"A franchise is basically the blueprint for a business that's already been successful somewhere else."

"Like a McDonald's?"

"Exactly. Only franchises aren't limited to fast food. You've got car washes, locksmiths, preschools, senior care, computer repair, financial services, insurance, construction services, and more. The list is endless."

"But the blueprint is going to cost me something, right?"

"Well, sure! No one gives away the secret to a successful business model for free."

"So how much?"

"It varies, depending on the complexity and name recognition of the business. You may be able to open a simple commercial cleaning franchise for several thousand dollars, whereas you'll need $250,000 or more for a McDonald's."

"If I had a quarter of a million dollars, I'd be rich already. I wouldn't have to hassle with a burger joint."

"You're not doing the math," challenged Roger. "At $25,000 of expenses per year, that $250,000 represents only ten years of 'rich' retirement. What then?"

Darn! Roger sure knew how to burst one's bubble. A quarter million dollars sounded like a lot, but in reality wouldn't fund too long a retirement on the Riviera.

"What then?" echoed Larry. "Back to work, evidently."

"I don't know about you, but I'd wish I had invested that $250,000 in a business which generated $50,000 in profits per year so that I could retire indefinitely."

"Yeah, that would work."

"But it doesn't work without putting in the work," cautioned Roger.

"I get it, I get it," groused Larry.

This hotel wasn't the only mark Benson left on the city. Portland was primarily a lumber town in the early 1900s and Simon Benson one of its timber barons. A teetotaler himself, he didn't approve of mill workers stepping out for a few beers during lunch. His solution was to install copper fountains, later to be known as Benson Bubblers, so workers could quench their thirst conveniently. Fifty-two iconic bubblers were still in operation in the downtown area today.

Given the responses so far, it seemed unlikely Larry was about to start a business of his own. Maybe it was time to highlight some of the benefits.

"Is your company a big place?" asked Roger.

"Not really, around 15 employees."

"No doubt you've met the owner?"

"Oh yeah. I went to lunch with him when I was interviewing for the job. We drove to the restaurant in his S-Class Mercedes. Now that is a fine ride."

"Probably a business expense," observed Roger.

"You mean it's not his?"

"Not necessarily. Why should he personally buy it when he can have the business lease it for him and write it off as an expense?"

"I'll bet the business paid for the lunch too," guessed Larry.

"For sure—recruiting is a legitimate business expense."

"The owner takes a trip every year to Maui. Says it's for a business seminar. He's not paying for that?"

"Probably not. Continuing education, market research, business meetings, and associated travel. Those are all expenses which can be charged to the company."

Larry saw that owning a business could have its advantages. But it was a big leap from employee to owner. The employee just did his job every day while the owner had responsibility for the whole shebang. And if it went south, couldn't the owner lose everything?

"I wouldn't mind having the company Mercedes," said Larry, "but what happens if the business doesn't make it? Won't I lose everything I own?"

"It depends on the legal form of your business."

"Legal form?"

"A business is a legal entity in the eyes of the state, and that entity can be defined different ways."

"Like a corporation?"

"Exactly. Other legal forms are the single proprietor, the partnership, the limited liability company (LLC), and others."

"That limited liability one sounds good. Will that cover me?"

"It might. But keep in mind that no legal structure will protect you from unethical behavior."

"Yeah, look at all the Wall Street fat cats being hauled into court these days," said Larry.

Often such a comment was all it took to sidetrack Roger into a rant on political malfeasance and Wall Street excess. But it didn't work today.

"Picking the proper legal structure for the business is the first big decision a prospective business owner has to make."

"But I don't know any legal stuff," objected Larry.

"That's where your coaches come in."

"I'm starting a business, not putting together an NBA team!"

"Your coaches are a small group of legal, financial, and other professionals who support your business plan and can offer advice as you get going."

"Where am I going to find people like that and why would they give me advice for free?"

"You've already done it in a way."

"I have?" asked Larry, unaware that he had done anything that smart recently.

"Sure. Haven't I been your personal finance coach these last few weeks?"

"But you're my uncle!"

"True. But I would have done this even if you weren't my nephew because I'm a caring guy and you're worth it. Besides, there's nothing finer than passing on experience and seeing it put to good use."

"So before I think of starting a business, I need to find a bunch of guys like you, only with legal, accounting, and business expertise?"

"You got it," affirmed Roger.

Larry fell silent as he realized how hard it would be to develop relationships with experienced professionals, convince them he had a good business idea, and solicit their advice. That required a level of maturity and goal-oriented focus which had eluded him in life thus far.

"Most businesses that fail do so because the owner isn't multi-dimensional. He might be good at one or two things, but that's not enough."

"Yet in the early days, the owner has to do it all himself," observed Larry.

"That's why your coaches are so important."

"I see how it works now," said Larry, "but it sure seems like a lot of serious effort."

"That's what it ultimately comes down to, Larry. How exceptional do you want to be?"

Larry was at his limit for today and made moves to leave. "Gotta go. Same time next week?" he asked.

"No. I'll be out of town for a few weeks. I've got some east coast marathons scheduled which my wife and I will combine with a New England tour to take in the fall colors."

"It must be nice to travel whenever you want," griped Larry, whose job inflexibility and budget barely supported two weeks off per year.

"Time to come up with a plan, then, and put in the effort to make it happen," replied Roger, who had heard the identical complaint from his own brother all too often. "It's your life."

"I'm in charge?"

"Oh, definitely!"

Roger's last words took hold as Larry headed out through the ornate lobby. Why couldn't he come up with a plan and stick with it? These sessions had given him enough background to get started. Now it was just a matter of desire. No more excuses. He'd write down some ideas, numbers, and timelines and review them with Roger when he got back from his trip. Wouldn't he be surprised? For all his uncle's eccentricities, the guy was right about one thing.

"It's my life and I am in charge!"

Epilogue

Dear Reader,

Kudos to you for making it this far. If you lack a natural interest in finance or don't have an affinity for mental math, you deserve an extra pat on the back. I'm honored that you stuck with me and hope you'll tolerate some final thoughts.

If you acknowledge that any topic can have at least two points of view, then it's possible that everything in this book is wrong. That doesn't bother me any as long as you continue your education—financial or otherwise. Seek out opposing viewpoints. You don't have to believe me. Rather, you need to believe that it's within your power to self-educate and decide things for yourself. That can be scary at first, but it's quite liberating once you make it a habit.

Don't underestimate the role luck will play in your life. For example, how lucky is it that you were born in an era and nation which value literacy and you're able to read this book at all? That's an example of completely random luck over which you have no control. Then there are the wonderful times when preparation meets opportunity. Luck provides the opportunity. You need to provide the preparation.

World events, government policies, political shifts, natural phenomena, and unnamed things we have yet to identify will influence your life in unpredictable ways. Get used to it. Become an expert at adapting.

Your life is a one-time experiment. Make it a good one.

Best wishes,
Dave Straube

###

Connect with me online at:

www.DaveStraube.com

Bulk Purchases

&

Custom Reprints

Someday Is Not a Plan is available in bulk purchases or as a custom reprint for organizations, corporations, clubs, promotions, and gifts. Special editions with personalized covers or organizational imprints can be created in quantity for specific needs. The publisher is especially interested in making this material available to financial literacy organizations in a format which complements their existing materials. For more information, write us at:

Island Eye, LLC
1500 SW 11th Ave.
Suite 2204
Portland, OR 97201

www.IslandEyeLLC.com

Made in the USA
Charleston, SC
01 July 2012